Sixty Years of Rifles
A Personal Odyssey

BY PAUL A. MATTHEWS

Manufactured in the United States of America

All rights reserved. No part of this book may be used or
reproduced in any manner whatsoever without prior
written permission from the publisher except
by a reviewer who wishes to quote brief passages
in connection with a review.

Queries regarding rights and permissions
should be addressed to:

Wolfe Publishing Company
6471 Airpark Drive
Prescott, Arizona 86301

Wolfe Publishing Company is not responsible
for mishaps of any nature which might occur from
use of published data in this book.

Wolfe Publishing Company
ISBN: 1-879356-03-1
Copyright © 1991

The author on the second day of buck season, November 27, 1984. The rifle he carries is his favorite Ruger No. 3 .45-70 with Lyman 48LEE receiver sight and 1/8-inch wide blade front sight.

Warning

This book contains loads, loading practices and procedures that I developed or used in various rifles over the past 40-odd years. Although these loads and procedures were apparently safe for the rifles I used them in and in the manner in which they were used at the time they were used, they may be dangerous in your rifle and may cause damage to equipment and/or personal injury. I have included these loads and procedures as a matter of information and not with any implied or specified recommendation. Neither I nor the publisher will accept any responsibility for injury or damage from the use of any load or loading procedure described in this book. If you choose to use the loads, or to follow the loading procedures described in this book, you are strictly on your own.

Paul A. Matthews
December 22, 1989

Dedication

To my mother and father who many years ago turned my footsteps in the right direction and filled my life with memories which will be cherished to the end.

Contents

Introduction xiii
1 The .22s 1
2 The .32 Winchester Special 25
3 The .44s and a .38-40 33
4 The .300 Savage 51
5 A Couple of Japs 57
6 The .30-40 63
7 The .30-06 75
8 The .375 H&H Magnum 91
9 The .45-70s 123
10 A .348 Winchester 151
11 The Model 92 .25-20 155
12 A Husqvarna .243 157
13 The .458 161
14 A New Model 1863 Sharps 169
15 The Lyman Great Plains Rifle 181
16 Odds and Ends 193

Introduction

Considering all of man's material possessions over the centuries, his personal weapons have continued to be the most cherished and the most likely to accompany him on that last trip into the Great Beyond. Indeed, up until the latter part of the nineteenth century, most men carried a personal weapon of some sort, whether it was a small pocket pistol for the city dweller, or a rifle or sidearm for the outdoorsman.

Today such practice is frowned upon by the idealists of society — it is abhorred by them. Those of us who do still believe in man's inherent right to possess, carry and use a firearm for protection of self, family and property, or for the practice of hunting, are looked upon with distaste as though we are contaminated.

However, have those social idealists ever owned a rifle? Have they ever personally used a rifle for self protection? Have they ever carried a rifle mile after mile through snowladen hemlock and laurel stalking the elusive buck? Have they ever studied a distant target and searched their brain for the correct formula of windage and elevation, confident that if they did their part the rifle in their hands would do the rest? Have they ever carried or used a particular rifle so much that that portion of the grip where the thumb rests is worn to a smoother polish than the rest of the stock? Have they ever seen the blueing worn from the floorplate, trigger guard or action merely from being carried?

This is a book about rifles, rifles I have owned or used, many of them with the blueing worn through and the stock polished from contact with skin or clothing. It is a book about an extension of my personal being, because at one time in my life I seldom left the house without a rifle, and never since earliest memory have I ever been without access to a rifle. Indeed, I've owned a rifle ever since that cold day on March 17, 1935, when the little Sears Roebuck single-shot .22 was passed on to me by my older brother Wilfrid.

Many rifles have passed through my hands since that day, most of the them are now gone because in my ignorance I didn't see their potential or know how to wring that potential from them. What I wouldn't give today to have a few of them back! Not being able to recover them however, I resort to mental recall to write of them as I once knew them.

One more thing. In the opening chapter there are some instances of game law violation, instances for which there is no justification regardless of the time and circumstances in which they occurred. I include them exactly as they happened to illustrate the way we used a rifle, the way my family thought of a rifle in those long bygone days. However, the recounting of these experiences should in no way be interpreted as condoning such behavior. Today there is no room for the game law violator, nor any justification for such actions.

Paul A. Matthews
December 17, 1989

1

The .22s

I stood on the edge of the field next to the hedgerow and watched the deer lope along the far side. I didn't know whether it was a buck or doe, nor at that time did I even care. In my child's mind, however, I knew with a certainty that the deer would run until it reached the newly hard-surfaced road bisecting the farms along the Sheshequin Flats, and that it would then retrace its route back toward the Buckhorn, running up the center of the 20-acre field. So positive was I of this that I ran out to the middle of the field, hit a prone position with the little Sears Roebuck single-shot and placed an open box of .22 Shorts within easy reach.

Just as predicted, a few minutes later the deer — a buck — came loping up the center of the field not 30 yards from me. With a methodical coolness not too common among kids, I pulled back on the striker knob, took steady aim and fired. Fifteen more times while that buck went past me, I worked the bolt, chambered a cartridge, took aim and fired. And after the buck was out of range, I lay there and watched him enter the fringe of brush on the hillside and disappear.

I headed for home on a dead run and a few minutes later was trying to shake my dad from his Sunday afternoon nap on the parlor davenport.

With sleep-bleary eyes he asked me what the problem was.

"I saw a deer," I said. "A buck. If you'd been there with the shotgun" (an old single-barreled Iver Johnson) "we'd 'a had deer meat for supper."

Dad grunted and rolled over, facing the back of the old davenport.

"I shot at it sixteen times," I ventured. "And it fell down up in the woods."

Dad came alive as if he had been jabbed with a hot poker.

"You what?"

I told him the whole story, growing more apprehensive as the words tumbled out and his face changed from a shocked pale hue to crimson and then to a mottled purple.

I've long forgotten his exact words, but the gist of the message was — after considerable discourse relative to the fact that it was Sunday and the day before deer season — that I wasn't going to get a new .22 for my birthday. I'd have to wait a few more years.

That incident happened in 1933 when I was but eight years old, and looking back on it, it's surprising that Dad didn't put the razor strop to use. In those days before Dr. Spock, more than one lesson was driven home and riveted over with the razor strop.

That little single-shot .22 was the sorriest excuse for a rifle I've ever held in my hands, but times were hard then and Dad had ordered the little rifle from Sears Roebuck in hopes that for less than $3 he would have a rifle with which to supplement the fare for the supper table.

The rifle was chambered for the .22 Short cartridge. It was a bolt action with a bolt knob no bigger than a pea. In order to cock it, you had to pull back on the striker knob. There was no safety and the sights were of the most basic sort. Even with all of these faults, however, the rifle might have had some potential if it had not been for the barrel, a brass tube wrapped with steel. If there was any rifling in that tube, it did little better than to keep the bullet's nose on the cartridge.

Now, Dad hadn't shot a .22 since he was a kid. He had always lived in town and moved to the farm in April 1925 in order to have some breathing room for an ever-expanding family. On the day the mailman left the rifle standing by the mailbox, Dad took it to the barn to try it out. He tacked a target to the side of the barn, paced out 30 steps and whaled away.

Right here you must understand that in those days we had never heard of a benchrest. Nor would we have used it if we had known such a thing existed. In those days a man shot standing on his hind legs. That was how a man hunted and it didn't make any sense to shoot a rifle any other way, even if you were trying to sight in. This remained our standard practice right until the early 1950s.

At any rate, it didn't take many shots before Dad determined that the rifle shot a somewhat tighter pattern than the old 12-gauge Iver Johnson, but it surely was no squirrel rifle. One other thing my dad learned that day was that .22 rimfire ammunition had changed a lot since he was a kid.

We had three Jersey cows in that barn, and when we went out to milk that night we found three of the bullets had passed just over the cattle and put holes through the windowpane on the barn's backside. How those cows weren't hit is beyond me, and we surely couldn't have afforded the loss of even one of them. Although the .22s of my dad's youth had barely penetrated a pine board to the full depth of the bullet, those of the 1930s showed considerably more spunk.

Later Dad borrowed a Remington pump from my cousin and from that day on fried squirrel graced the supper table almost every night. Sometime during the day he would ask my mother how many squirrels she wanted for supper. Whatever she requested, Dad went out and shot, no more and no less. He always shot them through the head.

The Sears Roebuck rifle became the property of my older brother Wilfrid. I was allowed to use it under close supervision and occasionally I was allowed to go hunting with Wilfrid if I remained at least three steps behind him and kept my mouth shut.

To the best of my recollection, only three pieces of game ever fell to that little rifle, the deer mentioned earlier, a squirrel and a duck. The squirrel came about one fall day while Wilfrid and I were hunting. The critter must have been feebleminded or bent on suicide, because it worked along the ground to within about five feet of us, a range short enough to almost guarantee a hit, but still too far away for precision placement.

Wilfrid hit the squirrel with the first shot, but the critter ran up a tree and from that point on I carried the box of cartridges, handing them to Wilfrid one at a time while he worked the bolt and fired as rapidly as possible. Somewhere halfway through the box of cartridges, he connected and the unluckiest squirrel in all of squirreldom tumbled down from the treetops — a perfect head shot!

March 17, 1935, was Wilfrid's fourteenth birthday and late that afternoon my dad presented him with a brand new rifle, again from Sears Roebuck. Stamped along the barrel was "Springfield Model 86 — .22 Short, Long or Long Rifle." Now this was a real rifle! Although it cost a bit over $10, which was a fair piece of change in those days, it was a man-sized rifle with a tubular magazine, a heavy bolt with a bolt knob the size of the government rifle, and a quality barrel that put the bullets where the rifle was pointed. Sighting equipment was the standard flat-topped open rear sight with a small U-notch, and a fine gold bead front sight. Although today we frown upon such equipment as being primitive, in those days we proceeded to kill game and bore tin cans just as though we had a scope.

As soon as Wilfrid had the new rifle in his hands and had cleaned the grease from the bore, I fell heir to the Sears Roebuck single-shot. Without wasting a moment, we pocketed a few cartridges and headed for the Susquehanna River that flowed not half a mile from the house.

At the spot where Mallory Run flows into the Susquehanna, a long stoney point juts out into the river creating an eddy of quiet water on the downstream side. As we approached the eddy, six or eight ducks got up. The rifle snapped to my shoulder and when I pulled the trigger, one of the ducks tumbled. In an instant I was in Gloryland! And Wilfrid hadn't even had time to fire his new rifle.

Obviously not wanting to waste a golden opportunity, I explained at great length about how I had aimed at that particular duck — this was long before I had ever heard the term "lead" or even knew the reason for it — and how the little single-shot required a special understanding. I have long-since forgotten all the virtues I heaped on that rifle, but we went home happy as larks, me carrying the duck and my head swelling with pride almost to the bursting point.

The facts are, however, that the rifle was a piece of junk. Its only redeeming characteristic was that the striker couldn't be pulled back until the bolt handle was in the full-down position. This one fact brings to mind another distant memory.

My dad had taken me on one of those late afternoon walks in hopes of picking up some game for the next day's supper. We walked up an old dirt road and into a pasture lot which bordered Mallory Run. The woods jutted into the far end of the pasture at a location where, back in the early 1800s, an old mill dam had held the creek back and furnished power for a mill. Only remnants of the ends of the dam remained and my dad and I sat there waiting for a squirrel or whatever. Dad carried his old Iver Johnson and I had the .22.

Sometime during our wait, Dad felt the urgent call of nature and, leaving the shotgun on the ground beside me, sought the dubious privacy of a nearby bush. It was about this time that a grouse strutted out in full view maybe 20 feet away and I tried to pull the striker back for a shot, but the damned thing just wouldn't pull! No matter how hard I tried, no matter how close that bird got to me as my heart pounded like a tom-tom, I couldn't budge the striker.

I looked over and saw Dad squatting behind the bush with a big grin on his face. I saw that big cock grouse strutting around with his tail fanned and the feathers on his neck ruffled out, but I couldn't pull the striker back on that little rifle!

Then the grouse flew and within seconds I discovered that the bolt handle wasn't all the way down. It may have lacked only 1/16 inch, but that was enough. All my dad said was, "Why didn't you use the shotgun?"

At that age I'd have rather gone without.

I got my first real rifle on November 4, 1937. This one was almost a twin to Wilfrid's rifle, but had some improvements that I always felt put it in a class by itself. First, the forearm was grooved on both sides to provide a better grip. Second, it was equipped with a fold-down open rear sight and a selective aperture peep sight. Third, the front sight had three different inserts — a post, a bead and an aperture. (Page 38 of the 1944 First Edition of the *Gun Digest* states that this was the Springfield No. 086, although I'm certain the barrel was stamped "86." However, the barrel was not drilled and tapped for a Weaver scope as stated in that publication.

Dad despised peep sights, always claiming there was too much room around them. He later tried one on a .300 Savage Model 99EG, but soon removed it. Although he tried his best to get me to use the open iron sights on my new rifle, I insisted on the peep sight and the aperture front sight. This was a superb combination for small game, as at 30 yards a squirrel's head just nicely fit inside the aperture front sight.

I shot a lot of game and varmints with that rifle. At that time crows were unprotected, as were most hawks and owls. There was even a bounty on goshawks and the great horned owl, and any time a kid could earn money by hunting, he sure was going to do it.

However wrong it may have been — and maybe it wasn't wrong at that time — the feeling in those days was that the only good hawk was a dead hawk. Although a lot of sentiment remains against hawks and the great horned owl, it would be dead wrong to declare open warfare on them today as I did when I was a kid.

Scattered around the country at that time were any number of the old native chestnut trees standing gaunt and gray, leafless and barkless from the ravages of the blight since about 1912. These eastern giants would be three to five feet in diameter and stretched skyward 70 to 80 feet to provide a perch from which the mighty birds surveyed the countryside. I can recall at least six of these old chestnut trees that stood on our property or just over the fence line, and seldom was there a time when there wasn't a hawk or party of crows perched in one of them.

For economical reasons, we used mostly .22 Longs. A box of Shorts cost 10¢, Longs were 15¢ and the Long Rifles were 20¢. Since the cartridge case for the Long was the same length as that of the Long Rifle, we considered it to be of equal power. Precision accuracy had not yet entered the picture except possibly in the hunt for gray squirrel, which demanded a head shot.

Many times I started out in the morning with a magazine load of Longs (17, I believe) to take a shot at some hawk in one of the chestnuts. Sometimes the bird dropped on the spot, but as often as not I would hear him whistle as he took off and flew to another perch half a mile away where he would sit and whistle and shriek until I made another stalk and fired the second shot. Often this would go on for three or four hours until the bird was either too heavy with lead to fly, or all of his blood had drizzled out the many perforations. Once I made a hit, however, I never gave up. I stuck with the bird until I was able to carry it home and mail if off to the Game Commission for the bounty.

As for crows, they were more difficult to get than the hawks. Smarter, I believe. I used to take my rifle to a stand of heavy hemlock that we called Iroquois Land. After I had hidden myself, I would start calling like a young crow. No, I didn't have a store-bought crow call; I didn't even know such a thing existed, I would just mimic a young crow until the big ones came flying in and finally made up their minds to land in one of those hemlocks.

I can't say that I killed a lot or crows that way, but the ones I didn't kill, I scared the livin' Bejesus out of! As a matter of fact, it got so that crows in the vicinity wouldn't respond to a call, any call.

I don't know how many rounds I fired through my Springfield .22 rimfire, but it had to number well into the thousands. When I traded the rifle sometime about 1949 or 1950 for two Japanese Arisaka 6.5mm rifles, the backside of the bolt handle was deeply grooved where it rubbed against the raceway in the receiver.

One of the most accurate hunting .22s I ever used was a Marlin 39A that my brother Ernie had taken in on a swap. We had a local hardware store and the proprietor's son handled the firearms and ammunition end of the business. I'm not certain that he always made a profit on the swapping transactions, or if he ever made a profit, because Ernie was always coming home with a spanking new rifle or handgun.

The 39A was brand new, and although it was equipped with the usual bead front sight and a U-notch open rear, it shot where it pointed. My eyes were on the better side of perfect and with that little rifle I could hit just about anything I aimed at and hit it where I was aiming.

Ernie brought the rifle home on a hot August day in 1948, and after he had confirmed the sight setting, handed the rifle to me. I looked around for a moment and then spied what I thought was an empty tar can that my dad had left beside the chimney on the ridge of the house roof. To this day I don't know whatever possessed me to do such a thing, except that the can looked inviting, too good a target to resist.

Thinking I would knock it off the ridge, I pulled up and shot. The can jiggled a bit, but stayed there. Before I could take aim for a second shot, a black spot appeared on the side of the can, quickly elongating as the sun-heated tar oozed out and flowed down the side of the can onto the roof. Fortunately it was a small can.

On December 31, 1948, I was laid off from work until April 17, 1950. During that time I picked up whatever odd jobs I could find — digging ditches, working in a sawmill, spreading cow manure at 25¢ a load — and supplementing our table fare with game whenever possible, just as my dad had done during the Great Depression. Thus it was that in March of 1949 I was along the river one day carrying the Marlin 39A when I saw a dozen or so wild geese standing on the stoney point where Mallory Run empties into the Susquehanna.

I knew the geese had seen me, so I turned my back and walked straight away, turning around about 30 seconds later to see that they were gone. Running back to the river's edge, I saw the geese were coming ashore about a half a mile downriver where there was another small point and eddy.

The thought of roasted goose was irresistible and I quickly left the river and walked downstream through the adjacent fields. A broad fringe of trees and undergrowth separated the fields from the river.

Reaching the point about where I thought the geese had come ashore, I got down on my belly and crawled through the brush to the lip of the riverbank and peeped over. There, about 40 yards downstream from me, serving as lookout on the outer end of the little point, was a large goose. I cocked the rifle, took a solid aim at the back of the head and pressed the trigger. The goose never flapped a wing, but merely tipped over into the swift current.

Now you have to remember that this was in the month of March. The ice had gone out only a week or two before and nightly temperatures were still well below freezing.

Water temperature couldn't have been much above 35 degrees F., but without any hesitation I left the rifle on the bank and swam out to retrieve my goose, still wearing my lace-up hightop boots, red leather cap and heavy Woolrich jacket. The Marlin had put the bullet exactly where I wanted.

Although I shot a lot of game and varmints with the .22 rimfire, I consider the .22 Long Rifle to be a barely marginal small game cartridge. I realize this is contrary to almost everything I have ever read on the subject, and that the .22 rimfire has been used at one time or another to take almost every type of game on the North American continent.

I've shot many squirrels with the .22 rimfire and as long as the shot was in the head the way my dad taught me, I had a dead squirrel. However, regardless of how good we are, regardless of how careful we might be in proper shot placement, there always comes a time when the bullet doesn't go where we want it, and a squirrel shot in the body with the .22 rimfire will get to a hollow tree almost every time. The .22 rimfire Magnum is as far superior on small game when compared to the Long Rifle, as the .30-06 is superior to the .30-30.

I abhor wounded game. Nor have I any use for those who purposely use the smallest caliber possible for taking game just to see if they can do it. When the deed finally is done, these people never talk about the agonizing cripples left behind, but only the one successful shot they made. We as hunters have a moral, if not legal, obligation to carry and know how to use a rifle of ample caliber to ensure a quick kill even when the bullet doesn't go where we want. To do otherwise is criminal negligence.

To this day I am haunted by the last critter I ever shot with a .22 rimfire. It was back in the early summer of 1949 and I was carrying the little Springfield looking for woodchucks. Quite often in the early summer I would get a young one for the pot.

I was working along the foot of a sidehill field when a chuck popped up out of his hole about 40 yards away facing me. As it had thousands of times before, the Springfield found my shoulder and scarcely had the sights settled on the chuck's head, when I pressed the trigger. Almost in slow motion the chuck sank back into his burrow out of sight. I knew I had made a solid head shot and that the woodchuck was probably dead within seconds, so I got a length of old barbed wire and worked it down the hole. I cranked it like a drain snake to tangle it with the chuck's fur, but it was no use — I couldn't retrieve the chuck from his burrow.

About two weeks later Ernie and I had reason to live-trap some chucks in that area, and right after an afternoon thunder shower I suggested we check the traps. Chucks often come out to feed right after a shower.

By chance I had set a trap in the burrow where the chuck had been shot two weeks earlier. As I approached the trap, I could see that it was snapped and that what appeared to be an old rotted hide partially rain-beaten into the mud was caught between the jaws. At first, I thought someone had deliberately put a piece of old hide in the trap, but as I bent over to lift the trap from the mud, this almost unrecognizable shape opened its mouth and hissed at me. It was the chuck I had shot in the head with the .22, wasted away to nothing but rotted hide and bones, still alive and full of fight, but unable to eat or drink for at least two weeks. That image is burned into my memory forever, and I vowed then to never again shoot at game with the .22 rimfire. We owe the lowest animal on the totem pole better than that.

Still, if we face reality, the .22 rimfire is an extremely popular round widely used for plinking, targets and small game. In fact it is used widely enough on small game so that some of its most staunch supporters have set about to improve the killing power of the Long Rifle cartridge. This is done by making a small file die to permit filing a substantial flat on the nose of the bullet. According to reports, this in no way impairs accuracy, but increases tissue damage to the game by at least 50 percent.

For those who want to make such a die, or have one made, take a piece of ½-inch diameter oil-hardening steel stock and bore a .226-inch diameter hole through it. Face it to a length of .875 inch. After hardening, insert a loaded .22 Long Rifle and file the point down to the face of the die, giving a generous flat that even without expansion will greatly increase the killing power over that of the roundnose. Those who have used such bullets claim that expansion is greatly enhanced, further increasing tissue destruction and killing power.

Sometime back in the mid-1950s, Ernie had Charlie Canoll build a .220 Swift on a Mauser 98 action, a heavy Douglas 26-inch barrel, Bishop stock, Jaeger trigger and a 16x Fecker scope. As I recall we used a 50-grain bullet backed by 37.0 grains of IMR-4320, and at 100 yards we could just about cover five shots with a dime. At 200 yards, if we could see a spot on a woodchuck's head the size of a quarter, we could kill the chuck every time. Much beyond 200 yards, however, the wind played havoc with the little bullet, and if there was wind, most woodchucks were safe.

The only centerfire .22 I own is a Ruger No. 3 .22 Hornet. I purchased this rifle during the latter part of 1974 with no particular reason in mind other than the fact that it was the first No. 3 I had seen and I wanted it. The barrel was drilled and tapped for the three-point adjustable scope mounts with the base-mounting holes located about 7¼ inches apart. Because of this, I didn't even consider a scope for the first few months, but did my plinking and target shooting using open iron sights.

Then one evening while I was poking around a box of spare parts and other goodies, I happened to pick up a Weaver base whose screw holes matched the rear set of holes on the Hornet's barrel. Within minutes I had attached the block and had mounted a Weaver K6 on a single ring. Such a rig isn't the most substantial mount in the world, but it worked nicely and the recoil of the Hornet is so negligible that it didn't shift the scope.

Once I had good sighting equipment, I started working with different bullets and loads, finally settling on 11.3 grains of IMR-4227 with a 45-grain bullet or 11.0 grains of the same powder with a 50-grain bullet.

Both loads would shoot close to one inch at 100 yards if the barrel was kept clean. Keeping it clean involved scrubbing it with a wire brush and solvent until there was *no* trace of metal fouling left. I have never owned another rifle where the barrel seemed to foul as badly as this Ruger No. 3 Hornet. When looking through the barrel, it appears as perfect as a mirror, but putting a wire brush through it after only one shot feels like dragging a tight patch through a badly rusted water pipe. Hoppe's Bench Rest No. 9 does a good job of removing metal fouling. There may be other solvents just as good, but since I started using Bench Rest No. 9, I've had no problem keeping a clean barrel.

Just before hunting season opened in 1975, I decided to use this rifle for small game and finally settled on 5.7 grains of Unique behind the 40-grain Speer bullet. This was a superb load and I used it for years before changing to 8.0 grains of 2400 with the same bullet.

I should point out that like most Rugers at that time, my Hornet had considerable freebore. Since the 40-grain bullet is so short and has to be seated well out in order to fill the freebored area, bullet shape becomes quite important relative to accuracy. The 40-grain Speer bullet filled the bill nicely as it has parallel sides and a short cone-shaped point.

Those freebored chambers on the Rugers gave a lot of people fits because they didn't know how to take advantage of them. Instead of seating the bullet out to almost kiss the rifling, thus increasing case capacity, they invariably seated the bullet to the depth required to function in a box magazine or clip. By doing so, the bullet has to jump a considerable distance before engaging the rifling and this does nothing to enhance accuracy. However, I personally like the freebored chamber on the single-shots and found that by seating the bullets out and taking advantage of the increased case capacity, I could get good accuracy at slightly increased velocities.

The first day I carried the Hornet in the squirrel woods I was using the Weaver K6 scope. It took only a few hours and one or two close-in shots at squirrels to learn that 6x is just about twice too much. It was fine if the squirrel was out 30 yards, but if he was in close about all I could see in a 6x scope was a big blob of gray.

That evening I removed the K6, replacing it with a K2.5 that has remained there ever since. I know that some people use and recommend a 4x, but I think this invites taking shots that are a bit iffy as far as making a clean kill, especially if the rifle is a .22 rimfire. With the K2.5 scope I soon learned that any time the crosshairs obscured most of the squirrel's head, the squirrel was beyond positive one-shot killing range.

Another thing I soon learned was to allow for the height of the scope above the rifle's bore on the close-in shots. With my small game load, I sight the rifle in dead center at 50 yards, but when the game is up close — 15 to 20 feet away — the bullet is below the line of sight. I don't know how many squirrels I missed that first year, or how many grouse I've missed since because I didn't compensate for the distance between the centers of the scope and the bore, but after more misses than I care to think about, I started judging distances. If a squirrel worked in close before a shot, I would put the crosshairs on the tips of his ears for a dead-center head shot.

I have shot the heads off a good many grouse with both my old Springfield .22 rimfire and my Hornet. Over the years I've probably missed as many or maybe more than I've killed because I didn't allow for the distance between the scope and the bore. A large portion of sitting grouse shots are taken up close and offhand, and in the tenseness of trying to make a good shot, it's easy to forget.

There is one other thing that most first-time small game rifle hunters overlook. All too often they get excited and shoot too soon. *When hunting squirrels with a rifle, never ever shoot at a moving squirrel.* Always wait until the critter stops. This usually is when he first recognizes that everything isn't as it should be, and he will sit up like a woodchuck or freeze in a solid position. That's the time to make the head shot.

Many times while hunting squirrels with the Hornet I've had to let half a dozen of them go past me without taking a shot simply because they didn't stop to look things over. Sometimes when they did stop, they were at the wrong angle to make a head shot without tearing up the off shoulder or body. I pass these up with no regrets as there's always another time.

I've taken well over 200 gray squirrels with the Hornet and I dare say over 95 percent of them were with head shots. I've also taken several grouse, rabbits, a pheasant and four turkeys.

When using the proper bullet, the .22 Hornet is probably the best turkey rifle ever developed. I know that today everyone reaches for the shotgun when it comes to turkey; for some reason they consider the rifle to be less than cricket. I don't know why that feeling exists. It wasn't always that way. If you take a walk back through time and read the turkey hunting articles in the *American Rifleman* of the 1930s, it was all rifles — the .25-20, .25-35, and a host of others. When the .22 Hornet was announced back around 1933, however, it was hailed as the best turkey rifle to ever come down the pike. Today, with the proper bullet, it still has my vote.

What is the proper Hornet bullet for turkey? It's one that expands without going to pieces. For those big magnificent birds a bullet is needed that will readily expand, yet give deep penetration and preferably complete penetration. This quickly rules out bullets designed for disintegration within a woodchuck's head or crow's body. It also rules out a full-jacketed bullet.

Shortly after the Hornet hit the market, some of the old-timers tried full jackets on turkey. Usually the turkey went flat at the shot and then got up and made off only to die later. I mention this particularly because Speer puts out a beautifully shaped 55-grain, .22-caliber full jacket that is easily stabilized at Hornet velocities in a barrel with a 14-inch twist — which many of the Ruger No. 3 Hornets had. I was never able to stabilize a 55-grain Spire Point from my barrel, but the roundnose Speer bullet handles superbly.

The best turkey bullet I've used thus far in the Hornet is the Speer 45-grain spitzer softpoint. On the turkeys I've shot with it, the bullet went completely through the bird with no indication of breakup, but with rapid expansion. On one turkey I took using a Hornady 45-grain Spire Point, the bullet completely disintegrated within the turkey. This might be fine on a small hen or jake, but when you get a large hen or an old tom up in the 16+ -pound class, more positive penetration is needed.

During next year's turkey season, I am strongly considering a 50-grain Speer bullet backed with 11.0 grains of IMR-4227. Not only will it give me the positive penetration I want for the big birds, but with my rifle zeroed at 50 yards with the squirrel load of 8.0 grains of 2400 behind a 40-grain bullet, it is right on at 100 yards with the turkey load. Other combinations require a different sight setting for each load.

One thing I've never had success with in the Hornet is the use of cast bullets. To my way of thinking, a good Hornet rifle should be able to duplicate the very best of the .22 rimfires with a cast bullet at similar velocities. I've watched my nephew Joe Piccolo take his Savage Anschutz and fire five shots at 50 yards that you could cover with a dime. As I mentioned earlier, some of the .22s I used years ago didn't have to take a back seat in the accuracy department. Yet, I've never been able to come close to such accuracy with cast bullets from my Hornet. Why?

My personal theory is that the base of the .22-caliber cast bullet is so small in diameter that the unavoidable imperfections caused by the sprue cutoff have an adverse effect. This is made apparent by examining the gas check after it is applied. Almost invariably there is an imperfection that never shows up in the thicker, more rugged gas checks for the larger calibers. Even where there is an imperfection on a larger caliber gas check, it usually is located immediately over the cutoff and never reaches the bullet base's edge.

To me this is more than a casting problem. I've cast bullets for over 40 years — thousands of them in a number of various calibers. With a good mould I can cast 420-grain .45-caliber bullets with almost perfect bases whose weight tolerance won't exceed ± .5 grain. I'm a slow caster, usually averaging about 75 bullets an hour, and after trying both the dipper and the bottom-pour pot (each for a number of years), I've returned to the dipper method. For me it is the most consistent.

Getting back to .22-caliber cast bullets, I believe the answer to good accuracy lies in a nose-pour mould. I have two nose-pour moulds in .45-caliber made by Richard Hoch, and the bases on bullets from these moulds are like a sheet of glass — they're perfect. I believe that such a base on a .22-caliber cast bullet would give accuracy close to the half-inch mark at 50 yards providing the velocity was about that of the .22 Long Rifle. Someday when I get a few extra shekels to spend, I'll prove it!

The author with his Springfield Model 86 .22 and a woodchuck. Picture taken about 1940.

The author with his Springfield Model 86 .22 and an owl that he probably chased for several hours before the final shot. Picture taken about 1941.

The Ruger No. 3 Hornet with a Weaver K2.5 in a single-ring mount.

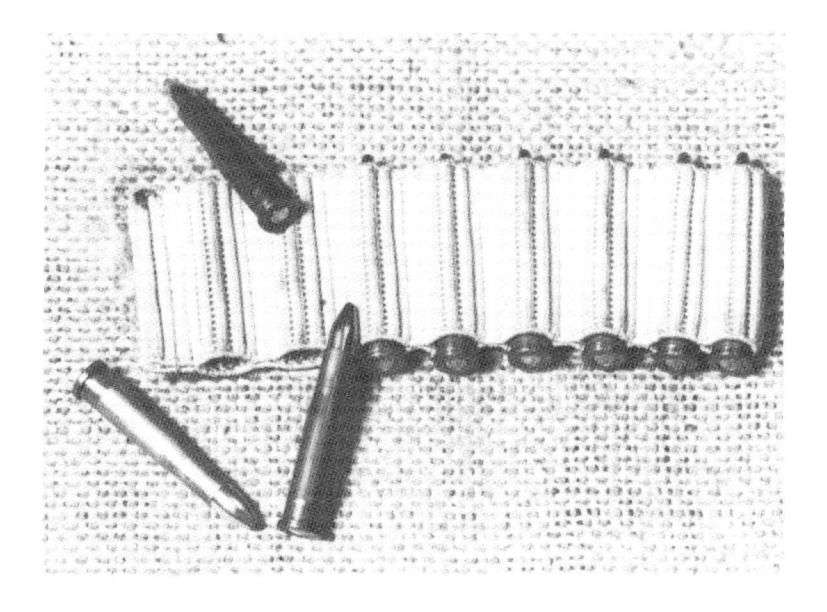

Hornet cartridges in a homemade elastic cartridge carrier. Carried in this manner the cartridges don't rattle and are not easily lost.

Large hen turkey shot with the .22 Hornet using a 45-grain Speer bullet and 11.3 grains of IMR-4227.

Waiting for squirrels in a soft drizzle. Load used in the Hornet is 8.0 grains of 2400 behind the 40-grain Speer bullet.

2

The .32 Winchester Special

On Monday, November 27, 1939, about 7:15 A.M., I squinted down the barrel of a Winchester Model 94 .32 Special carbine and sent a 170-grain Silvertip toward my first six-point buck. To this day I don't remember aiming at that buck, although I undoubtedly did. At any rate, it dropped in its tracks about 40 feet from me, its spine shattered.

That little .32 Special was my first high-powered rifle. Early that spring my dad gave me a newborn calf to raise and tend to, and that fall he bought the calf back from me for whatever sum I needed to bring my financial balance up to $27.75, the price of the rifle from Sears Roebuck and Company.

This was one superb rifle, though at the time I had no knowledge of its potential nor did I know of the reasons behind its development. I only knew that I had a real deer rifle and that I had to have a peep sight on it. So that November for my birthday my folks gave me a Lyman 1A tang sight that was promptly mounted and shimmed on one side so that it stood perpendicular to the bore instead of diagonally.

Trying to take things one step further, Dad drilled and tapped the bottom side of the front barrel band to take a sling swivel. Then he tried to slide the band back near the forearm, but found that doing so stressed both the tubular magazine and the barrel, so he put it back where it belonged and left it alone. I didn't want a sling anyhow.

At that tender age, I was not all that great a shot with the .32 Special. Reloading ammunition was something I had never heard about, and practice with a high-powered rifle was limited to three or four shots on the day before deer season. All other practice was limited to the .22 rimfire, something in which I have never believed. That is, I have never believed that you can become an efficient shot with a high-powered rifle through extensive practice with a .22 rimfire or any other smaller caliber.

If you are going to become proficient with the .30-06, then you had better do considerable shooting with the .30-06. It's permissible to start out with reduced loads in order to acclimate yourself to the rifle, but sooner or later you have to grab the bull by the horns and work with full-throttle loads. I don't know how many different shooters I've met over the years who were downright superb with the .22 rimfire on the indoor range. Hand them an '06 and many of them would refuse to shoot it, preferring to use the lightest practical caliber possible for their deer hunting.

I can't believe that I am the only rifleman affected in this manner, but I remember only too well that when I got my first .30-06 it took me months of shooting to master the recoil, and all of the .22 shooting of my past hadn't done one thing except to impress upon me the fact that the '06 was more gun that I had ever handled.

Naturally, the recoil of the .32 Special is considerably less than that of the '06, but nonetheless the jump from the .22 rimfire to the short, dogleg stock of the .32 Special carbine was, by today's terms, a quantum leap. I doubt that I fired half a box of ammunition through that rifle before I shot my first deer with it. In fact, I seriously doubt that I fired five full boxes of ammunition in that rifle during the whole nine years I used it. Yet, it was a very accurate rifle, far more so than most people ever gave it credit for.

I recall coming home on leave from the Pacific early in 1945, and the first thing I did was to pick up that rifle and take a poke at the bottom of a tin can wedged in the crotch of an elm tree 60 to 70 yards away. Standing on the back porch of the old homestead, I centered that can offhand and it stayed in the crotch of that tree until it rusted away. What I wouldn't give to go back and do that again!

That rifle made four one-shot kills on deer. The first was the buck mentioned at the beginning of this chapter; the second was another six-pointer that was running straight away from me up a sidehill pasture. The shot was offhand and the front bead was placed just under the root of his tail. At the shot, the buck piled up like a sack of wet cement.

On the first day of doe season in 1947, Dad, Ernie and I hunted in the vicinity of the old lumbering town of Laquin. I had made several claims that morning on our way in that I was going to shoot the biggest doe on the whole mountain. As far as I know, I did.

There was a good snow on the ground and I was pretty well bundled up in my Navy winter gear, so for the first hour or so of the morning it was my intent to sit. With a sweep of my arm, I cleaned the snow from an old three-foot diameter log and sat down. Not more than 15 or 20 minutes went by when I saw a string of doe, five in all, working through the timber behind me. The first two were yearlings and I let them pass. The third one in line looked like one of Dad's Jersey cows and I planted the 170-grain Silvertip just over the foreleg about halfway up the body. She made two jumps and piled up.

An hour or so later while I was sitting beside the deer warming my hands over a small fire, Ernie came by carrying Granddad's Colt Lightning .44-40. Ernie took one look at the massive size of the doe, laid the old .44-40 across her flank, and snatched up the little .32 Special.

"Gimme that gun," he said, and without another word he went tromping off through the woods out of sight.

A short time later I heard the .32 bark again and a half-hour after that Ernie came back dragging a chunky button buck. One shot, one deer. Ernie later told me he had to thread that bullet a long ways through the pole timber.

If I could redo or undo any one thing in my life, I would go back to that day in 1948 when I traded my .32 Special for an H&R 922 revolver, and bring the rifle back home again. Of all the rifles I've owned and fired in my life, that one deserved far more attention than it ever received.

Back in those days all the gun experts could (and did) quote you line and verse about how lever actions were so springy that cartridge cases had to be full-length-resized each time before reloading. More than that, the lever actions weren't all that accurate to begin with, and the only way for a real rifleman to go was with a bolt gun. Heaped on top of all this bull dung was the emerging claim that the .32 Winchester Special wasn't really all that accurate; that once the barrel showed a bit of wear, accuracy went to hell in a hand basket. It's not uncommon to see those same words in print today.

Instead of analyzing and comparing known facts as I do today, however, I fell under the influence of such sage-flavored baloney and dumped my .32.

So strong was this thinking that those in the know took advantage of we who were less knowledgeable and relieved us of some of the best deer rifles to ever part a laurel thicket. My brother Wilfrid had a .32 identical to mine, and one evening he told me that a man at work (an old backwoods hillbilly) had offered to trade a home-sporterized 1917 Enfield .30-06 for the .32 plus $10 to boot.

Now home-sporterization meant the removal of all excess wood and the application of several coats of varnish to what was left. In all honesty, the barrel of the Enfield was perfect, but when you consider that they were available from the DCM (Director of Civilian Marksmanship) at that time for about $8.50 plus shipping, the swap was no great deal for my brother.

We went to see the other half of the swap that evening, discussing pros and cons as we drove and reiterating all the bad things written about the .32 Winchester Special. Now, Wilfrid's rifle was newer than mine and probably hadn't had more than 50 rounds put through it, but the old hillbilly knew a thing or two, and when he noticed a slight hesitation on our part, he stuck a loaded cartridge in the muzzle of the barrel and flatly declared the barrel was worn out from cleaning — the cartridge dropped in all the way to the mouth of the case without the bullet ever touching the lands.

Wilfrid and I looked at each other. We did clean our guns often — didn't we? But we used a pull-through instead of a cleaning rod to avoid damage to the muzzle. Wilfrid blinked and I blinked. The evidence was there; the barrel was either worn out or never had been any good. The swap was promptly initiated without our ever checking any other .32 Special to see just how the bullet end of a loaded cartridge fitted the muzzle end of another barrel, or to see if it really had been a .32 Special cartridge or a .30-30. All the way home we congratulated ourselves on getting rid of a clunker when in reality we had been had by an old hillbilly woods stalker who knew a few things that the armchair, type-pounding experts hadn't taken the time to check out or explain.

Let's look at some facts. To begin with, the .30-30 and the .32 Winchester Special use the same basic case, and ballistically there isn't enough difference between the two cartridges to poke in your ear. Both shoot a 170-grain bullet about 2,200 fps, giving the .30-30 the edge in sectional density and the .32 the edge in bullet diameter.

Today, those who really know their gas checks when it comes to cast bullets recognize the .30-30 as one of the most accurate production cartridge cases available. The limited case capacity allows nearly 100 percent loading density for good ignition, and the long neck covers all of the grease grooves without having the base of the bullet protrude into the powder chamber. For those who have graduated to the paper patched bullet, my friend Charlie Canoll loads a very soft 177-grain paper patched bullet over 32.0 grains of IMR-4320 for an average muzzle velocity of 2,195 fps. That's a shade more poop than a factory load! I should also mention that Charlie is doing this in a Remington 788.

Now let's take another look at the .32 Special. This has the same cartridge case with the same powder capacity and same long neck as the .30-30. Most importantly, however, the .32 Special was developed especially for those old-timers who for many years had used the .32-40 and wanted a similar new cartridge that could be reloaded with cast bullets and either black or smokeless powder. In short, the .32 Special was designed especially for cast bullet shooting even to the extent of putting a gentle 16-inch twist in the barrel, the same as the .32-40, as opposed to the 12-inch twist of the .30-30.

Now I can't make claims for something I never did, but when I look back and read of the accuracy of the old .32-40 and note the cast bullets available for that cartridge and the .32 Special, like the Lyman 321297, I could kick myself all around the lower 40 for ever letting go of that rifle. In hindsight, I believe the .32 Winchester Special had the potential for being the greatest cast-bullet hunting cartridge ever developed, and the fact that it did not survive was through no fault of its own.

Doe taken in 1947. Left to right: Dad, Ernie and myself. Note that the doe on the right is a head and neck longer than the other two. She was a big deer!

3

The .44s and a .38-40

I can barely remember Grandfather Goble. Although he wasn't much of a hunter (at least my mother never mentioned him as a hunter) the old gentleman knew a good cartridge when he saw one. More than that, he had a taste for fine rifles even if such possessions were limited to only one — a Cold Lightning pump gun chambered for the well-established and reputable .44-40.

Actually, having but one rifle wasn't uncommon back in those days. Men bought the one rifle they thought would do the job, and they learned that rifle. Whether they realized it or not, they became aware of its trajectory, its accuracy and its terminal performance — the bottom line in their book. If the rifle worked out as planned, there was never a need for another. The Colt .44-40 worked fine for granddad because as far as I know it was the only rifle he ever used.

Grandpa Goble died in June 1931 and the rifle was passed onto my Uncle Frank who lived in Dover, Delaware. Because the city fathers frowned upon firearms within the city limits, however, the rifle eventually came back to a daughter and reposed for some time (years) in the upper rafters of an outdoor woodshed. That's where we found it on Sunday, November 30, 1947, the action immobile and the exterior of the barrel speckled with rust. I'm certain that had granddad seen it, he would have bawled.

Liberal doses of Hoppe's No. 9 applied with patches of soft flannel and considerable elbow grease gradually removed the rust and loosened the action so that it functioned like a wooden paddle in a bucket of grease. The magazine plunger was loosened so that cartridges could be stuffed in the long, underslung magazine, and the old rifle began to act like a thing alive.

I've long forgotten at what range we sighted in for, and can only guess that it was somewhere between 50 and 70 yards, and that that probably wasn't far from where the sights had been adjusted half a century earlier than Granddad first got the rifle.

At any rate, the next morning (the first day of the 1947 buck season) we crowded into the old '37 Ford and took off for Laquin, the remnants of an old lumbering town. This day was my brother Allan's debut to deer hunting, the first day of many to follow, and he was using the old Colt .44-40. Dad had his .300 Savage, Ernie was carrying my .32 Special and I was using my liberated Japanese Arisaka 7.7 with a chrome-lined barrel taken brand new from an arsenal in Japan.

Allan was only 14 at the time, that intermittent age between boyhood and manhood, an age when he looked to his elders for advice and help, an age when he was afraid of doing something wrong lest he banish himself from the family circle of deer hunters. Most of us have been there, and those who haven't don't know what they've missed.

On top of the mountain by daylight, we established our headquarters beside a huge granite boulder where we always built a fire and where the youngest of the party usually stayed on watch. The woods were vast and we were always concerned about someone getting lost before they learned the country. It was the same spot where I had shot my first buck back in 1939.

I loaded Allan's rifle for him. I stuffed eight of those short, fat cartridges into the magazine telling him that if he needed more than that, he didn't deserve a deer — even though the full-length magazine held 14 cartridges.

Ernie and I poked around the woods quite a bit that day, and about two o'clock in the afternoon were in a dense swampy thicket that stretched downhill on the far side of the mountain. We were slowly making our way back toward the granite boulder when the fusillade started, a single shot followed by seven more rolled out so fast they blended almost into one.

I looked at Ernie. "There's only one rifle on this whole mountain that will shoot that fast." I said. "That's Allan with the .44-40!"

About that time six more shots ripped out like a canvas sail tearing in the wind and we quickened our pace in working uphill toward the boulder.

When we got to our headquarters, there was Allan with a grin on his face second to none, and a buck with the most magnificent eight-point rack I've ever seen. His first shot went right where it should, in the boiler room. The buck went down but floundered and flopped on the ground trying to get back to its feet while Allan emptied the magazine and then stuffed six more cartridges into it.

I've long forgotten just how many shots hit that buck, but I do remember that there were quite a few trees in the area that had fresh splinters anywhere from two feet off the ground to 10 feet over my head! I've read since that with the Colt Lightning cornshucker, all one had to do was hold the trigger back and work the slide. That may well be true; I never tried it and the old rifle is now long gone to God knows where. If it is true, however, I suspect Allan came pretty close to doing just that on his first day of deer hunting. He wasn't taking any chances!

The .44-40 and its kid brother, the .38-40, were two very remarkable cartridges. The .44 probably killed more two- and four-legged game than any other cartridge before or since. It was used the world around, from Alaska to Tierra del Fuego, and it killed game that today we would hesitate to tackle with anything less than a belted magnum of some sort. The facts are, however, that in the heyday of the .44-40, men hunted on two feet, not from a tree stand or 4x4, and they worked in close and put that fat little slug right were it belonged on the first shot. That made the difference.

Back between 1903 and 1913, the old *Hunter-Trader-Trapper* magazine published a series of experience recollections written by E. N. Woodcock, a Pennsylvania trapper and market hunter from about 1862 to shortly after 1912. Before the days of market hunting were over in Pennsylvania, it wasn't uncommon for Woodcock to shoot between 20 and 30 deer during the month of December plus a few bear he had trapped. His preference in hunting rifles was the old Winchester 1873 chambered, as he stated it, for the .38 Winchester — the .38-40

Having to tramp miles a day on a trapline, many times making overnight camp in the woods, these old trappers and market hunters wanted an easy-handling rifle that could hold a lot of short, stubby cartridges firing a chunk of lead big enough to do the business whether or not it expanded. The .38-40 and .44-40 filled the bill nicely.

Sometime during the early 1950s I picked up a Marlin 1889 .38-40 with a 26-inch round barrel and a full-length underslung magazine. This little rifle had been specially made to order for someone, as the forearm and grip were checkered and the buttstock was a fine piece of wood with a high comb and cast-off slightly to the right. The barrel had a few shallow pits, not too bad, and the action had more than enough headspace, as the primers backed about a quarter of the way out. All in all, it was a beautiful little rifle but again, in my ignorance, I didn't know what I had nor how to use it.

The problem was the barrel and the jacketed bullets with which my cartridges were loaded. At 50 yards, any semblance of accuracy was a sometimes thing, groups usually were measured in terms of six to eight inches. Looking back on it, it's surprising that accuracy was even that good because after pulling one of those jacketed bullets and dropping it in the breech, it fell all the way to within two or three inches of the muzzle where a gentle push on a wooden rod shoved it on through, barely showing marks of the rifling on the soft jacket. The fact that the barrel was loose at the breech and tight at the muzzle didn't register with me, nor did it ever occur to me that if I bought a good mould and cast some soft bullets, I would probably have had an excellent black-powder rifle.

Later I sold that Marlin for $5, half of what I had paid for it. I was ashamed to take that money because the gun wasn't accurate, but the man who bought it was happy. From his back porch across an adjacent dirt road he could hit a 40-quart milk can every time!

Sometime in the late 1960s, or early 1970, my brother Ernie purchased one of the new Marlin 1894 carbines chambered for the .44 Magnum. Now this was something I should have sunk my teeth into, but didn't because I was busy purchasing a Ruger No. 1 .375 H&H and later some No. 3s. More than that I wasn't overly enthused about the Marlin Micro-Groove barrels or the 38-inch twist they put in the barrel.

In spite of all these things I didn't like about the new Marlin, Ernie and his sons started taking a deer or two every year with the .44. As I recall, all of the deer were doe at ranges something less than 50 yards, and it seldom took more than one shot to do the job. There were two that had to be tracked down because the bullets were placed too far back. We were able to trail one on snow, but we had to track the other animal about a third of a mile on dry leaves through hemlock and laurel. When we came upon her half or three-quarters of an hour after the shot, she was down for the count.

This performance was in sharp contrast to a couple of shots I had made with the '06 years earlier using Jack O'Connor's favorite load of 52.0 grains of IMR-4320 and a 150-grain Remington bronzepoint bullet. With those two deer the blood trail petered out and even on snow I couldn't keep the tracks separated from other deer.

I don't have to be hit in the head twice with the same two-by-four in order for something to sink in, so along about the middle of 1973 I purchased a rolling block .44 Magnum of Spanish manufacture at a price I couldn't refuse. The little rifle had an 18½-inch barrel, a sad excuse for open iron sights and a handiness about it that made me wonder why everybody didn't have one.

After working with the rifle for a few weeks, I had some decent iron sights installed and purchased an RCBS 44-240-SWC bullet mould. I also purchased a Lee mould for a roundnose bullet and borrowed a couple of Lyman moulds for the Keith-style bullet (one of the moulds being hollowpointed). Regardless of bullet or load, however, the rifle didn't shoot the way I wanted or expected.

Then came the eye-opener — or eye-closer, as the case may be. I had fired about 800 rounds through that rolling block when, on January 28, 1974, my son George drove in the yard with his wife and family. Within a few minutes after his arrival, I had the rifle in hand and a pocketful of ammunition loaded with 22.0 grains of 2400 behind the RCBS bullet.

As we headed out across the yard, I noticed a pair of inflated balloons that George's kids had released from the car and which were now blowing across the sidehill behind the barn. Quickly I snapped off a shot and one of the balloons disappeared. I reloaded, took aim at the second balloon and fired. At that instant my head exploded and I went down.

It took 10 stitches to close the rip in my eyebrow and seven more stitches by one of the best eye surgeons in the country to sew up my eyeball. In the process, a bit of the cornea had to be removed so that today my shooting eye is over 50 percent pupil, irregular in shape and no longer dilates. I spent eight days in the hospital, and yes, I was wearing impact-resistant glasses. Without them, my eye would have been gone.

Examination of the action parts showed that the breechblock had a heat-treat crack in it. The extent of the crack was obvious because when the part was blued, the blueing seeped into the crack. Memory says that the crack covered about 20 percent of the total fracture, which speaks well for the rolling block action. Even with such a long crack, the breechblock had stood up for about 800 rounds. It is my understanding that shortly after the accident, all of these rifles were recalled. I've never seen another one.

At any rate, once I had tried the .44, I caught the .44 fever, only this time I wanted a Marlin. So one May 5, 1974, I visited Creekside Gun Shop at Holcom, New York, and purchased a Marlin 1894 Sporter with a fairly heavy 22-inch barrel and a half magazine. This was a mansize rifle and it handled beautifully. Even before shooting it, I installed a Lyman 66LA receiver sight and later a fluorescent bead front sight.

Unfortunately for Marlin, the marketing manager who established the design specifications for the new Model 1894 hadn't paid attention to shooters' requirements or was totally out of touch with the reloading game and cast bullets. The first error (shallow Micro-Groove rifling) could be tolerated. It's a form of rifling that gives good accuracy although velocities with soft bullets must be held to around 1,400 fps. Why in the world Marlin every elected to put a 38-inch twist in the barrel is beyond me. Then when Ruger produced the No. 3 chambered for the .44 Magnum, they followed suit and did the same thing! I firmly believe that had the two companies used a barrel with a 20-inch twist and conventional rifling, their sales would have at least doubled if not trebled. Anyone who uses a .44 handgun or rifle is almost of necessity a bullet caster.

Despite the shortcomings of the rifling and twist, to say nothing of the undersized bullets — .429 and .4295-inch diameters by our jacketed bullet manufacturers — I fell in love with the Marlin. In a short two years I put over 6,800 rounds through that barrel, mostly the RCBS bullet backed by 10.3 grains of Blue Dot.

Today I have but three loads I use in the Marlin, loads that at 50 yards are all close enough so that a change in sight setting is not required for casual work.

For a cast bullet load, I use the RCBS bullet cast hard and backed by 5.0 grains of Bullseye. This load has a very soft voice, is deadly accurate and produces a velocity of about 915 fps.

For a deer load using a jacketed bullet, I use the Speer 240-grainer backed with 22.0 grains of 2400 for a chronographed velocity of 1,680 fps. Quite a few of the deer that Ernie and his boys shot with the .44 were taken with this load.

Since I personally doubt there is much expansion with jacketed bullets in the .44 Magnum, my own preference for a deer load would be the heavier 265-grain Hornady bullet backed by 22.0 grains of WW-296 for an average velocity of 1,541 fps. Even at the reduced velocity, I believe penetration with the heavier bullet would be better than with the 240-grain Speer.

Now a few paragraphs back I made reference to some of the jacketed bullets being as much as .001 inch undersize. To get top accuracy from the Marlin 1894 with the shallow Micro-Groove rifling, jacketed bullets must be a full .430-inch in diameter. All of the Remington 240-grain bullets I ever used and some of the Hornady 265-grain bullets were of this diameter, but most of the others (Speer, Sierra and some Hornadys) always miked .429 or .4295-inch and never quite delivered the accuracy of the larger bullets.

When using Speer bullets, which have a fairly soft jacket, I used to roll a second cannelure on the bullet, thus squeezing it up to .430-inch. This helped accuracy. Another thing that helps accuracy in the cast bullet department is to use the correct size expander plug. Most pistol loads need a lot of bullet pull in order to achieve proper ignition and complete combustion within the revolver cylinder. Thus, the expanding plug for pistol ammunition usually is about

.425-inch. However, with a soft bullet, or let's say unless you are using Linotype, the bullet diameter is likely to be reduced a few thousandths when forced into such a tight neck. This certainly isn't conducive for accuracy in a rifle. Maybe the pistoleers can handle it, but I can't.

An expanding plug for rifle ammunition should measure about .428-inch, enough to exert a firm grip on the bullet without distorting it.

If I could have but one gun — rifle, shotgun or pistol — with all of the reloading accessories and components to go with it, I would have to take a long, hard look at the Marlin 1894 Sporter or carbine. Now you must understand that in making this remark, I'm speaking for myself and the way I hunt in Pennsylvania. Most of my hunting consists of prowling the woodlots and thickets for deer, turkey and small game, although Pennsylvania is known for having the nation's largest black bears. In my hunting, however, I do little sitting; I'm usually on my feet, and for this a person needs a lightweight, easy-handling rifle.

More than that, however, the .44 Magnum cartridge is extremely versatile. Many writers equate it with the .30-30 because of its similar energy figure, and thus rate it as a 125- or 150-yard rifle. No way! Forget the energy figure and look at the bullet. It is a short, fat bullet of modest velocity. It has neither the sectional density nor the ballistic coefficient of the 170-grain .30-30 bullet. At its very best, the .44 Magnum cartridge from a rifle is a 75-yard cartridge, and in my book, that's stretching it. However, within 50 yards, as the old-timers proved with the .44-40, the .44 Magnum with either of the two deer loads mentioned and the bullets properly placed, is a superb firearm for deer or wild hogs. In fact, for wild hog shooting where the work often is done in close and dogs are a concern, the .44 Magnum is almost unimpeachable.

If I had to, I would go after black bear with the .44. I believe the .44 Magnum would handle a blackie in the 100- to 150-pound class, but when we start looking at bears from 200 pounds and up (a few years ago they shot one in Pennsylvania that topped 700 pounds) I want my .45-70 with heavy loads.

The Marlin 1894 Sporter chambered for the .44 Magnum also is a superb small game rifle. When Marlin announced that they were chambering the 1894 for the .32-20, I started looking for a way to raise a few shekels to obtain one of those rifles. Since I couldn't raise the funds right then, I took a look at my .44 and about the middle of the 1988 small game season took it squirrel hunting. I used the RCBS 44-240-SWC bullet cast hard and backed with 5.0 grains of Bullseye.

Since I was using iron sights, a Lyman receiver sight with a fluorescent bead up front, the rifle carried easier than my Hornet with its scope, and I no longer had to allow for the height of the scope over the rifle's bore. No matter how near or far the squirrel was, I held dead on.

The rifle and load proved superb on small game. Although it doesn't shoot the tight groups that the Hornet shoots, most small game taken with a rifle is shot within 30 to 50 feet, not yards, and for this the .44 is extremely deadly. After using it for one day just to try it out, I carried it for the rest of the season.

My bullets were quite hard, about 14 BHN as tested on the LBT bullet hardness tester, and every squirrel I shot was a head shot. When I picked the first squirrel up from the ground, it appeared as though there wasn't a mark on it. Whereas the Hornet pretty well took a squirrel's head apart, my .44 bullet merely punched a clean hole through the head, shattering the skull to mush and letting the perforation in the hide close up again.

When squirrel season opened in 1989, I reached for the .44 instead of the Hornet and even gave strong consideration to using the .44 with my squirrel load on turkeys. However, because there would be no expansion and because I had read too many old reports of shooting turkeys with full jackets — albeit with much smaller calibers — I vetoed the idea and used the Hornet with a 45-grain

Speer bullet backed by 11.3 grains of IMR-4227. The fact remains, however, that anyone who has a Marlin 1894 chambered for the .44 Magnum has a superb small game rifle.

I should mention that in addition to the Lyman 66LA receiver sight, I also installed a Merit Iris Shutter Hunting Disc. This device works like a camera shutter and lets you open or close the aperture of the peep sight to accommodate various lighting conditions in the woods. It is not a gimmick. When I carried the rifle in the fall of 1989, I had a number of gray, cloudy days when I opened the aperture to its maximum. On sunny days I closed it down, bringing the front sight into sharp focus for my tired old eyes.

Not only is the Marlin .44 good for deer and small game, it also can be used with the Speer shot capsules and No. 9 shot loaded over 10.0 grains of Unique for killing snakes or taking frogs. The pattern isn't as dense and uniform as with a .410 shotgun, but it will do the job, and you'll go a long ways before you can find tastier fare than fresh frogs' legs fried brown in butter, salt and pepper!

I know of no other cartridge that works as well as the .44 Magnum, and no rifle better adapted than the Marlin 1894, for covering such a wide variety of uses. Yes, if you're going to hunt deer with the .44, you've got to get in close and put the bullet where it belongs, and you won't need an oversized 3x9x scope to do that. In fact, putting a scope on the little .44 is somewhat akin to putting a speedometer on a lawn tractor — so much extra baggage!

The prize buck of a lifetime. Brother Allan with the buck he shot in 1947 using Granddad's Colt Lightning .44-40.

The Marlin 1894 Sporter chambered for the .44 Magnum and equipped with a Lyman 66LA receiver sight.

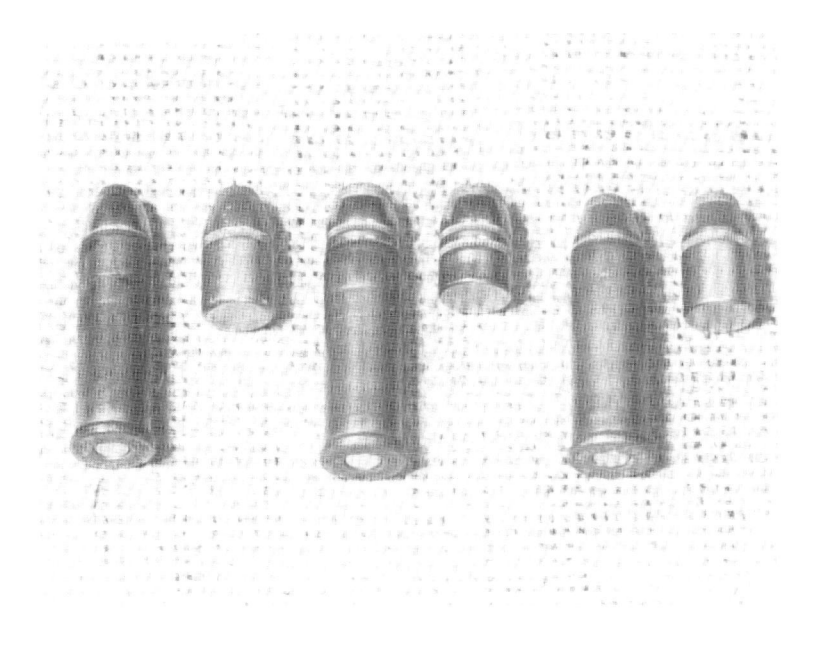

Some .44 Magnum cartridges loaded for deer. Left to right: the 265-grain Hornady bullet, the 240-grain Speer with an extra cannelure rolled in to seat the bullet out farther, and the Sierra 240-grain hollowpoint.

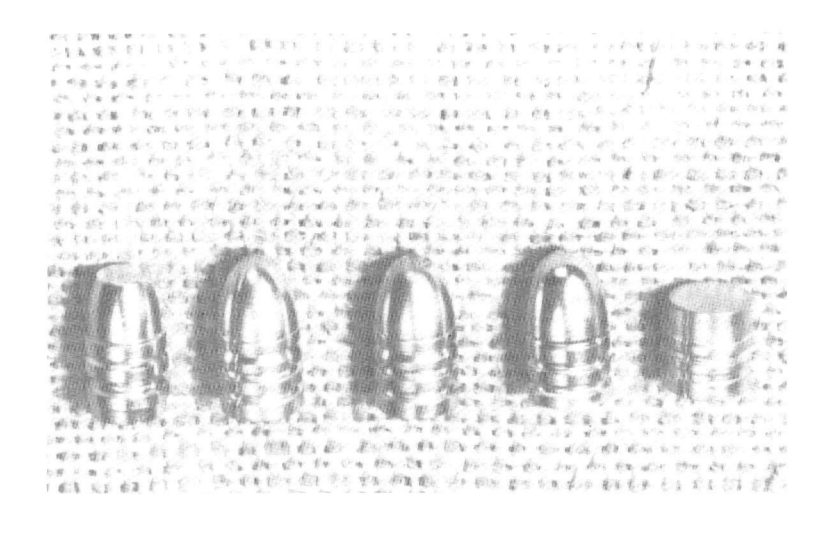

Cast bullets for the .44. Left to right: the RCBS 44-240-SWC, Lyman 429251, Lyman 429251 flattened on the nose so that it will feed through the action, Lee 429-240-2R and Lyman 429352. The RCBS bullet backed by 5.0 grains of Bullseye makes a superb load.

Speer shot capsules loaded with No. 9 shot, superb for snakes or frogs.

The Marlin .44 Magnum makes a handy hog rifle. Although the author prefers his .45-70, the .44 serves as a good spare rifle.

4

The .300 Savage

One incident will forever remain etched in my memory. The year was 1949, the month was December, and the day was antlerless deer season in Pennsylvania. My dad and I were hunting in the mountains at Laquin and, about two o'clock in the afternoon, were working our way along a high ridge. I was dragging a large doe I had shot earlier and Dad walked about 10 steps ahead scanning the hardwoods and scrub pine on the slope and bottoms below.

Suddenly he stopped and across the expanse of frosty air, I heard him say: "Here's where I get my deer!"

The .300 Savage Model 99EG swept to his shoulder in one easy motion. Looking in the direction the muzzle pointed, far below us (so far they looked like animated toys) I saw two doe scurrying for safety amongst the pines and hardwoods.

The rifle snarled once and Dad worked the lever with a flick of his wrist. It barked again and in a simple matter-of-fact voice, he told me: "I got that last one!"

Leaving my dad on the ridge to guide me with hand signals, I worked my way down the slope until I got to where I thought the deer had been. Then looking back at Dad, he motioned straight ahead by holding his arm straight up. In this fashion he walked me to the spot where he had last seen the deer. Not 20 feet beyond lay the doe, two holes through the chest close enough together to cover with the palm of my hand.

I've never matched that kind of shooting — offhand with a semibuckhorn rear sight and a Sheard front on a lever action that isn't supposed to be all that great in the accuracy department. This shooting was from a man who in his whole life didn't shoot as much ammunition as I've shot in the last two years, but that was my dad, my dad with the rifle he cherished using 180-grain Western Cartridge Company Silvertips.

Back in the 1930s money was tighter than an onion peel and just about as thin. Broken window panes were stuffed with wads of newspaper and tarpaper often served as linoleum. We cut firewood every weekend using a six-foot, two-man crosscut saw with my dad on one end and one of us boys riding the other end. Three Jersey cows gave us butter, milk and buttermilk, and along about Thanksgiving or New Year's we always butchered a hog or two. Other times of the year we raised a one-acre garden, picked wild blackberries by the pailful and raised a couple of hundred chickens for eggs and a different taste of meat.

Despite our never going to bed hungry, money was scarce and my dad wanted one thing above all else — a Savage 99EG chambered for the .300 Savage cartridge — $43.50 at the local sports store. Three or four different times during the 1930s he had squirreled away pocket change for a period of months until he had almost enough, and each time a family emergency ate up his savings.

He finally reached his goal, however, and in the fall of 1937 came home from town one day with a Savage 99EG wearing a nice piece of burled walnut on the back end. Dad let me take the first shot through that rifle and I can remember yet that I thought the trigger pulled awfully easy. He used that rifle from that day until sometime in 1964 when he passed it on to my brother Ernie. During those intervening years Dad shot a number of deer, most of them with one shot. Since 1964, Ernie has kept up the gun's reputation.

Although I never particularly liked the short neck and sharp shoulder of the .300 Savage cartridge, I always have believed that its velocity and bullet structure were at an optimum balance for deer and black bear. The 180-grain bullets from the .300 Savage always were light enough in structure to expand on deer regardless of the range. At the same time, the 2,400 fps velocity wasn't so severe that the bullets disintegrated at close range. You can't say that for a lot of other .30 calibers (including the '06) which start throwing their 180-grain bullets at 2,700+ fps.

This bullet structure business, something few people ever studied or examined in the past, has caused more cussin' and discussin' than anything else I know. The average hunter just never could get it through his head that there is a vast difference in bullets and an equally vast difference in requirements, and that these differences increase directly in proportion to velocity increases.

Today we have several bullet makers, Nosler among the better known, who manufacture bullets especially designed to accommodate the differences at higher velocities. Even with the regular commercial bullets, some of the ammunition makers have tried to educate the shooting public as to which bullet should be used for a specific game animal.

A few years ago Winchester offered Cartridge Selectors for those who were interested in using the proper bullet. The selector listed a .30-06 180-grain Silvertip as an elk, moose or brown bear bullet, while the .30-06 180-grain Power Point was designed for antelope, deer and black bear. I don't know how many hunters paid any attention to this, but I recall several times back in the 1940s and 1950s when neighbors shot clean through their deer with '06 180-grain Silvertips and the bullets never opened up one bit.

Getting back to the .300 Savage, however, as I said its velocity is in just about the right bracket to provide bullet expansion without breakup from the muzzle out to any decent range at which a man should be shooting. In fact, somewhere I read or heard from someone who had plenty of gray matter between their ears, *that, after you reach a velocity of about 2,500 fps, if you want more killing power, you should go to a heavier and/or larger diameter bullet instead of higher velocity.* This makes a lot of sense, assuming of course, that you are using a bullet designed for 2,500 fps and not 3,000 fps or faster.

I don't know how many deer my dad shot with the .300 Savage, but it had to be at least two dozen. I don't recall that he ever missed a deer with it, and I'm dead-certain that he never hit one that he didn't get.

Now after 52 years of action, the old rifle has developed considerable headspace. A factory cartridge can be fired once, but if the case is resized and reloaded, it will separate on the second firing every time. To circumvent this problem, I made up several cases from .308 brass and sized them to a crush fit in the chamber. These have been reloaded several times with no sign of incipient fracture. Because accuracy has begun to deteriorate in the old rifle. I seat the 180-grain Hornady roundnose bullets out a bit until they are just shy of the rifling. This makes the rifle a single shot as the cartridges don't feed properly, but accuracy is about 1¼ inches for three shots at 100 yards, and that's good enough for any deer. As for the single-shot business, one good first shot is worth a dozen of the other variety! That old .300 has proved it many times!

Spike buck taken by Dad with his .300 Savage in 1955.

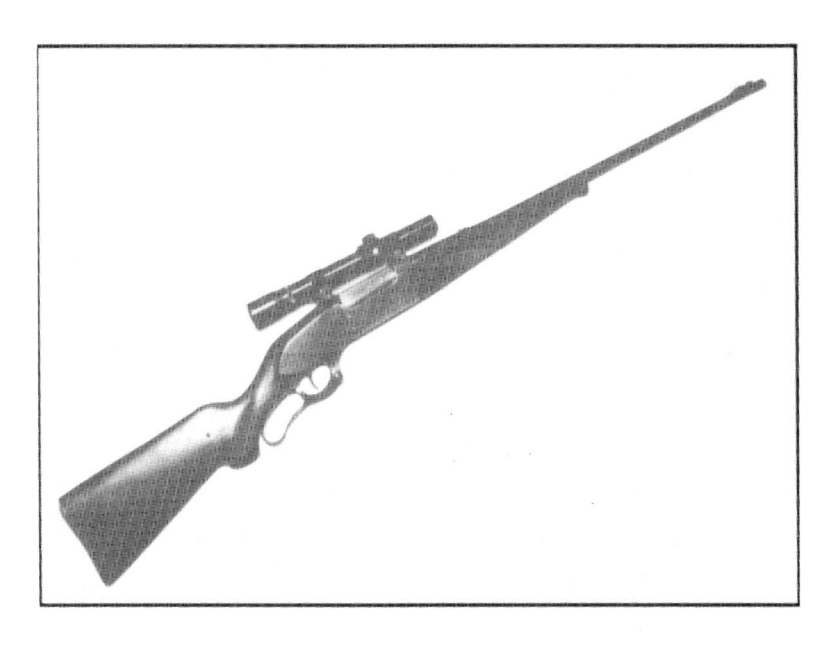

Allan's .300 Savage. The grip and comb on this rifle are shaped just a bit different than on Dad's rifle.

5

A Couple of Japs

When the spoils of war were divvied up in September or October of 1945, every man aboard our ship received a Japanese pistol, bayonet or rifle according to his rate or rank. Our division officer, knowing my liking for rifles, saw to it that I got a brand new 7.7 Arisaka with a chrome-lined barrel. Of course, at that time the term "seven point seven" wasn't used, at least amongst those of us who were ignorant. We called it a "Thirty-one Jap" or a "Twenty-five Jap" depending upon the rifle in question.

Now in those days everyone who ever put pencil to paper knew that the Japanese didn't know how to build a good rifle. The rifles were pieces of junk using feeble cartridges that could barely kill a man, but easily punched holes through the sides of our tin cans — destroyers — anchored off the coast of some jungle-covered South Pacific island. What other nation was so simple-minded as to produce a bolt assembly comprising only six parts (if you count the claw extractor and its keeper), and that could be disassembled in less than three seconds? What military of any intelligence would ever consider chrome-lining the barrel to protect it from the ravages of high humidity and salt air? To the best of my knowledge, the Japanese were the only ones foolish enough to do such things.

In all fairness, there were some Arisaka actions machined from castings instead of forgings, and these were totally unfit for anything except scrap. But on page 10 of Parker O. Ackley's *Handbook for Shooters and Reloaders,* he states: "The Jap 6.5 action was the big surprise of the tests. The indications are that this action is the strongest one that will be tested, regardless of origin or make."

The rifle I brought back from the war was brand new with a top-quality action and barrel, and in the fall of 1947 I made up my mind that despite all the doom and gloom writings about the Jap rifle, I was going to kill a deer with mine.

Ammunition and ignorance were major problems, and not necessarily in that order. "Thirty-one Jap" meant nothing to me. As far as I knew it could be just another designation for the .30-06 or .300 Savage or .32 Special. I didn't know, so I went to a neighbor who always had a knack for such things and who had a cigar box full of more different cartridges than I knew existed.

One by one we checked the bore size by stuffing a loaded cartridge bullet end-first into the muzzle of my Arisaka. The 8mm Mauser didn't seem to go quite far enough. The .30-06 seemed to fit about right in the muzzle, but wouldn't go all the way in the chamber. As he checked one cartridge after another, my brain whirled at a screaming pace. Maybe the .300 Savage....

With some small degree of caution mixed with a smidgeon of common sense, I ordered 10 military cartridges for the Jap 7.7 from Philip Jay Medicus of New York. I don't recall the price, but the cartridges were quickly forthcoming and I went to the cow pasture with five of them. The first shot missed the target completely and, since no one else was present, I cheated on the second shot by leaning against an apple tree to help steady the rifle.

The total results of those five shots are long forgotten, but the results of the sixth shot are indelible. The .300 Savage cartridge came to mind again, and since no one else was there to witness a disaster should that occur, I went to the house and came back with a single cartridge from Dad's horde. It was a bit shorter than the Jap cartridge, but the bullet end seemed to fit the bore about the same and it chambered without a hitch. So with no further thought, I pulled up and fired.

Everything held together and the cartridge sounded normal. If I hit the target, I've long forgotten where, but the brass case I ejected looked more like a brass shotgun shell with a bit of turn-down on the mouth than it did a .300 Savage. That was no problem, however, because I hadn't yet considered such a thing as handloading or reloading ammunition. What I did consider was going to town to buy a box of .300s to use for the forthcoming deer season!

Before continuing, I want to emphasize that this was an extremely dangerous thing to do and could easily have resulted in my getting seriously injured. To begin with, the rear of the Arisaka chamber is larger in diameter than the head of the .300 Savage or the .30-06 — although there were a lot of Japs rechambered for the '06 and a lot of 7.7 ammunition made from '06 cases. Although this didn't seem to give much trouble, a brittle case could have split and wreaked havoc with both the rifle and shooter.

More important, when using the .300 Savage cartridge in the 7.7 chamber, the only thing that held the cartridge against the firing pin was the claw extractor. In short, such a cartridge/chamber combination results in excessive headspace that can be measured in whole fractions of an inch instead of thousandths of an inch. Under such conditions it would be very easy to have a complete case separation and turn a lot of high pressure gas loose in the action.

Don't, under any circumstance, attempt to fire a .300 Savage cartridge, or any other cartridge except a 7.7 Arisaka, in an unaltered 7.7 Arisaka rifle.

Now in those days it was common for those who had a military rifle to use military ammunition for hunting. The more knowledgeable shooters filed the points back to expose a lot of lead to promote expansion, while the less knowledgeable left things as they were and bored pencil-size holes through anything and everything that got in the way. I was about halfway in between. With my last five 7.7 cartridges, I filed the tips back until I could just see a pin prick of lead and then went deer hunting.

Those five cartridges lasted about an hour. On that frosty morning in 1947, two different bucks sailed past me to God knows where, and as far as I could determine, I never touched a hair. Then I went to my dad and borrowed a magazine load of .300 Savage cartridges.

"Will they work all right?" he asked.

"Yep," I said. "I've tried 'em!"

Fortunately I didn't see any more bucks. That was the last time I ever fired my war prize, and sometime in 1948 or 1949 I sold my Arisaka 7.7 to Charlie Canoll who set the barrel back and rechambered it to .300 Savage. A new bolt handle was installed, a scope was mounted, and that piece of Japanese junk started punching out groups that hovered right around the one-inch mark, something that not many production rifles did in those days.

When I made my next acquaintance with a Japanese Arisaka, I had a bit more knowledge and had just entered the realm of handloading. I was out of a job and had swapped my .22 Springfield for two good-quality Arisaka 6.5s. The excess wood was trimmed off and the remainder treated with a mahogany stain and several coats of varnish. I gave Ernie one rifle and he paid to have them both rechambered to accept the .257 Roberts case. We purchased some 156-grain 6.5mm bullets from Norma and were in business.

That particular Norma bullet represented what I always considered to be the optimum design for woods deer hunting. It had a mild steel jacket that peeled back like a banana skin without breaking off, and the entire nose of the bullet (almost back to the origin of the ogive) was exposed lead. Such construction guarantees expansion at a very modest muzzle velocity out to as far as any man ought to be shooting at a deer, and the sectional density and weight of the bullet ensures deep penetration from any angle. Even on chucks, those heavy bullets perform beautifully.

The 6.5x257 was an excellent little cartridge. At that time I still didn't know how to work up a load, nor had I yet built a benchrest. Sighting in and serious shooting was done from the prone position. Still, I got by without blowing my head off, although when I look back at some of the powder and load combinations I put together, I shudder at what the consequences might have been had it not been for that special Providence that takes care of children and damned fools!

There was a lot of talk and a number of articles being written at that time about using Kirksite or zinc alloy bullets. Western Alloy Company of North Hollywood, California, started producing zinc alloy bullets for various calibers, and they could be purchased with a copper plating or left plain. The plated bullets looked better, but I don't recall that it made any difference as far as function or performance was concerned.

Zinc alloys (at least some of them like Kirksite and Zamak) have a self-lubricating characteristic and do not require a grease or wax-based lubricant like a lead alloy bullet. They leave little or no metal fouling in the barrel and can be driven to the full velocity capacity of the cartridge and rifle. They are very hard — Kirksite A had a Brinell hardness of 100 — giving absolutely no expansion, and having a nasty tendency to ricochet when striking at a shallow angle as often happens when shooting at woodchucks.

The zinc alloy bullet weighs about 60 percent of what a lead bullet from the same mould would weigh, and is about the most miserable thing I can think of to cast. Yet, I've read that some of the old-time African hunters often tempered their muzzleloading balls with zinc to help prevent distortion and assist in penetration. After having cast and used many zinc alloy bullets myself, and in view of all the recent hype about the new ultra-tech solid bullets that sell for an arm and a leg, I'm wondering just how long it's going to take some enterprising young genius to come up with mass-produced, zinc-alloy, African solids.

In my brief notes on the 6.5x257 Arisaka, I mention using a 78-grain Kirksite bullet in front of 20.0 grains of 4759. I have no idea of what the velocity was, but my notes say it was a very mild load and it easily shoved bullets through an eight-inch hemlock at 60 yards. I do recall recovering one of those bullets and the only deformation was that made by the rifling. This particular bullet was purchased from the Western Alloy Company and was the same design as the Cramer bullet mould No. C-1. It had a long, bore-riding nose, semi-spitzer point and two driving bands.

Most of the Kirksite bullets offered by Western Alloy were of the Cramer design, and looking back on it I suspect those bullets were less prone to stick to the mould than a bullet of the Pope design where the entire length of the bullet body is a series of driving bands and grooves.

For some reason I never recorded the grouping ability of the 6.5x257 with the Kirksite bullets or the Norma 156-grain bullets. I guess it all amounted to the fact that in those days I was more interested in hitting what I was aiming at instead of grouping my shots close together.

The smallbore Arisaka didn't stay in my rack too long. My wife Betty carried it for deer one year, but since she is left-eyed and has to shoot left-handed, the rifle was awkward for her to use. Besides, I wanted something new to play with, and in time the Arisaka went to town and became part of a swap on a Winchester Model 71 .348.

6

The .30-40

The boar was trotting across my front making the pole timber flicker past the scope like a picket fence. Then the hog came to the trail we had just come up and, instead of crossing, he turned and headed toward me. In an instant I put the crosshairs between his deep-set beady eyes and sent one of Hornady's finest on its way.

The cartridge used that day in the Smokey Mountains of Tennessee was the venerable .30-40, and the rifle used was a Ruger No. 3. Back in 1948 Ruger was just coming over the horizon and I had to have another rifle to replace the .32 Winchester Special I had so foolishly traded for an H&R 922 revolver.

At that stage of the game I was just beginning to look into the business of handloading and cast bullets. I had ordered the 1943 edition of the *Belding and Mull Handbook* (reprinted in 1947) and the *Ideal Handbook Number 35* (printed in 1948), both of which I devoured, digested, spat out and then chewed up for a second, third and fourth time. Anything I found that mentioned reloading ammunition, I read until my eyeballs lifted the print off the page. The faults of the lever action were apparent, although men had been reloading for them for years. One other thing was mentioned numerous times: A rimmed cartridge case did not shorten from case head to shoulder with light loads as did a rimless case. I didn't understand it all then, but it was grist for the mill and I chewed on it.

Sometime late that summer or early fall during one of my trips to town, I peered through the glass storefront of a secondhand shop and stared at the short-barreled bolt action rifle inside. Minutes later — or maybe it was seconds — I was snapping the carbine to my shoulder, squinting along the barrel at an imaginary buck and noting that the top of the front sight was bent sharply to port. A piece of white paper tucked inside the breech and held to the light while I peered down the muzzle showed that the bore was dirty, and not wanting to hurt the proprietor's feelings by asking for a cleaning rod, I said: "How much?"

"Twenty dollars."

The exchange was promptly made and I headed for home, stopping long enough to purchase a box of cartridges and proud as punch that now I was in the league of real riflemen. I had a bolt action. More than that, it was chambered for a rimmed cartridge which, when I got to handloading, had a distinct advantage over the rimless cartridge.

There is a lot to be said for a rimmed cartridge. Although most shooters today strongly favor a rimless or belted cartridge, the latter of which actually is an extended rim, it is the substantial rim that provides positive headspacing, prevents shortening of the case when using light loads, and eliminates the problem of misfires as a result of setting the shoulder back while full-length resizing. Although the last is not always a problem, I have known of instances of full-length resizing .35 Remington cases to such an extent that they wouldn't fire in a Marlin 336 lever action. The cartridge slid too far forward in the chamber to be reached by the firing pin.

As for whisper loads, especially in the .30 caliber, these are superb for small game and plinking, or shooting at a time when you don't want to raise a ruckus. When using a whisper load in a rimless case like the .308 or .30-06, however, the force of the primer often drives the case forward in the chamber with enough force to actually set the shoulder back and create excessive headspace. Although excessive headspace may not be a problem with whisper loads, if these shoulder-shortened cases are reloaded with full-throttle loads, then one runs the risk of separated cases and high-pressure gas running loose in the action. However, all of this was still in the future for me.

At home that evening a cleaning patch was shoved through the amputated barrel, giving the distinct feeling of rubbing the hair on a dog the wrong way. Once the crud was removed, I could easily see that the barrel was pitted from end to end, the rifling dark and not all that distinct from the rest of the barrel. Still, I liked the way the rifle handled and, using a pair of pliers, I straightened the front sight only to find out later that the previous owner had purposely bent the sight to make the rifle shoot where he looked.

In the process of removing the barrel and action from the stock, a small brass shim fell to the floor. I had no idea of where it came from until I reassembled the rifle and discovered it now had a two-stage trigger pull instead of the single-stage prior to disassembly. The previous owner had placed the shim under the front of the trigger guard, took the slack out of the trigger letting the shim fall back against it, and then tightened the guard screws.

Despite a home-applied instant blue job that left the barrel a blue-milk color, and a two dollar install-it-yourself peep sight with nut and bolt adjustments, my dad was totally unimpressed with the Krag. Nothing I could say about its ballistics being equal to that of the .300 Savage or the marvels of the side-box magazine where all one had to do was dump in a handful of cartridges, made the slightest dent in his opinion. He merely turned the rifle over in his hands, studied it a moment and handed it back. The expression on his face was either one of deep sadness or utter futility. I have never been able to determine which.

During the next day or two I took the rifle behind the barn and, leaning against the apple tree to help steady things, proceeded to find out for myself that a good hit on the target was a sometimes thing.

Since that long-ago day I've shot other rifles whose barrels' interiors looked like a discarded water pipe, and more than once I've been surprised at the fine accuracy such barrels can deliver. However, back in that day in 1948, not yet having graduated from the apple tree to the prone position, there was no way I could really determine whether the rifle would deliver any kind of accuracy or not. I sighted it in as best as I could and went deer hunting. I hadn't even reached the top of the mountain before I had a standing shot at a buck and missed him clean as all outdoors.

This was like getting hit in the pit of the stomach and before that deer season was finished I had made up my mind that I was going to buy a good rifle, a brand new Winchester Model 70 .30-06. The Krag was sold for $20 and the money went as partial payment on the new rifle.

I have always had a love for the Krag, especially the original carbine with its short easy-to-handle overall length. Back in the 1930s and 1940s it was a very popular cartridge in the Pennsylvania deer woods, and I believe most men used the long 220-grain bullet which some swore shot perfectly flat. A lot of them killed their deer to prove it.

Like the .300 Savage, the velocity and bullet structure of the .30-40 are balanced to give optimum performance on deer. On the bigger stuff, the long, heavy 220-grain bullet at a modest velocity always gave reliable expansion, deep penetration and good weight retention. In the cast bullet department, the .30-40 again was the ideal with a long neck to support a heavy bullet while covering all the grease grooves without letting the base of the bullet extend into the powder chamber.

In reality, the advantage of the long-necked cartridge case is most apparent under hunting conditions when spare cartridges are sometimes carried in the pocket.

Under these circumstances, exposed grease grooves pick up dirt and grit — not the best things to be running through a rifle barrel. Although I strongly favor long-necked or straight-walled cases, there are a lot of knowledgeable cast bullet shooters out there doing things with the .308 Winchester case that will knock your socks off in the accuracy department.

However, there is a vast difference in requirements of cast bullets used to fire tight groups off the bench and cast bullets used for deer hunting. Where bullets for the former usually are cast of a hard alloy and then heat-treated to make them still harder to be driven at a fairly high velocity, the only cast bullet the deer hunter should ever use is one that is soft enough to expand out where it hits without breaking up. By necessity this means lower velocity, and when you are dealing with lower velocity, the heaviest bullets available for that caliber deliver more horsepower on the far end and usually are more accurate. Heavy bullets, cast or jacketed, are right at home in the .30-40 cartridge case.

That was why, in 1976, I purchased a Ruger No. 3 chambered for the .30-40, and why, when the store owner remarked that it was too bad the rifle hadn't been chambered for the .308, I merely smiled. Had it been chambered for the .308 Winchester, I wouldn't have bought it.

My No. 3 .30-40 is an exceptionally accurate rifle. In fact, I've never heard of a No. 3 .30-40 that wasn't an exceptionally accurate rifle. Although I've never carried it deer hunting, it usually is sighted in and ready to go as a spare.

One Sunday while Charlie Canoll and I were putting the final touches on our rifles in preparation for the opening day, I put five shots downrange that made a cluster barely large enough to accommodate the tip of my little finger. Granted, it was a fluke group, but the rifle will shoot.

My Ruger No. 3 .30-40 is another rifle that, like my Hornet, must have a clean barrel in order to deliver that gilt-edged accuracy with jacketed bullets. It is not as difficult to keep clean as the Hornet, but the operation must be done to keep the barrel free of fouling.

I strongly suspect that if the truth were known, there is an overwhelming number of rifles out there that don't even approach their best accuracy because of metal-fouled barrels. Many shooters never give it a thought. They shoot all day and that evening make a few passes at the bore with the cleaning rod, then put the rifle away for next time, never aware of the fact that the extent of their cleaning has only cleaned away the powder smoke.

In March 1979 Lyle Jackson and I were sighting in our rifles in preparation for a wild boar hunt in Tennessee. Lyle was going to use his Winchester Model 70 Mannlicher chambered for the .30-06 and I was using my Ruger No. 3 .30-40. Now Lyle was an experienced rifleman and hunter, having shot in local competition and having hunted in Africa, Alaska, Canada and the western states. He had an enviable collection of antique arms as well as some fine modern rifles, and he knew how to use them.

Lyle's Winchester, however, wouldn't shoot for sour apples. He was using the Hornady 165-grain bullet backed, as I recall, by 49.0 grains of IMR-4064. He had used the rifle for a number of years, always sighting it in on my bench and always a bit displeased at its three-inch plus groups. He had even called Winchester about the rifle's accuracy and had been told that if it would shoot a three-inch group at 100 yards, he should be satisfied. Lyle wasn't satisfied, but liked the way the rifle handled and so resigned himself to its mediocre accuracy.

While walking back toward the bench after shooting his final group, I asked Lyle if he wire-brushed the bore of his rifle on a regular basis.

"Yep," he said. "Every year after deer season's finished, I make one or two passes through the barrel with a wire brush, then oil 'er up and put 'er away."

I never tried to explain anything to Lyle, but just reached over, took his rifle and headed for my gun room. While he stood watching, never uttering a word, I darned near wore out a wire brush on that barrel. Then without any comment, I picked up a clean target and five cartridges and went back to the shooting bench. The five bullets made a ¾-inch center-to-center group and all Lyle could say was: "I never would have believed it if I hadn't seen it!"

The boar hunt in Tennessee was an eye-opener. Lyle shot the first one, a 150-pound animal that was coming toward him at a slight angle. The 165-grain Hornady struck at the base of the neck on the right side, traveled the length of the hog and lodged under the hide on the backside of the right hind leg. The boar never faltered, but turned, giving Lyle a chest shot which promptly put the hog down.

Half an hour later I planted a 220-grain Hornady round-nose bullet between the eyes of a 200-pound boar, dropping him like a wet dishrag.

"You better hit 'im again," the guide said.

But I shook my head no, confident that the lights had been turned off for good. I did reload the rifle and just stood there for a moment to make certain the hog was dead before approaching him. Seconds later, one of his front feet twitched and then the other one, and then both hind feet got into motion and my "dead" hog got to his feet. I laced him with a second 220-grainer through the chest, and this time he went down for good.

One thing is for certain — wild hogs don't kill easily. If they can get at you, they can do a lot of damage with their razor-sharp tusks. As my brother Allan puts it, a hog's nervous system is all screwed up. It's like a fine network of wires with none of its ends attached to carry the message "Hey, I'm dead!" from the brain to the rest of the body. Many times, when I was a kid on butchering day, I've watched my dad throw a hog and stick it, and then watched the hog get to its feet to feed on an ear of corn while its lifeblood gushed out the sticking wound.

With an animal like that, energy figures are so much Madison Avenue fluff on a sheet of paper. What is needed is a large diameter bullet that gets rapidly larger with expansion and then has enough weight to push it through muscle and bone, damaging a lot of tissue on its way.

The load that I used that day in Tennessee and the load I shot the tight group with was 48.0 grains of IMR-4350 behind the Hornady 220-grain bullet. Although I never chronographed that load, Bob Hagel (in *Rifle* No. 48) listed an average velocity of 2,442 fps with 50.0 grains of IMR-4350. That is a shade better than the factory .30-06 load which is listed at 2,410 fps at the muzzle!

Before continuing let me point out that these loads are far too excessive for any .30-40 rifle except for the Ruger No. 3, and even in that rifle they should be approached with caution. Let me also add that my 48.0-grain load shows no indication of excessive pressures; primers are still rounded and the empty cases are easily extracted from the single-shot rifle.

Being able to achieve these ballistics from the Ruger No. 3 single shot is made possible only by the long neck on the .30-40 case and the freebore ahead of the chamber in the barrel. When seating the 220-grain bullets in the .30-40 case, I seat them out $\frac{5}{32}$-inch farther than normal to get the ogive of the bullet close to the rifling origin. This means that the base of that long bullet is not even close to the bottom of the case neck, thus providing additional case capacity, something that cannot be done with the short-necked .308 case. Indeed, if a 220-grain bullet is seated in a .308 case, the base of the bullet protrudes into the powder chamber so far as to cause considerable reduction in case capacity.

Shortly after purchasing the Ruger No. 3 .30-40, I bought a pair of bullet moulds, the Lee C309-180 and the RCBS 30-180-FN. Both moulds cast a fine bullet and both have a gas check shank. The nose on the Lee bullet is about halfway between a truncated cone and a roundnose, while the RCBS sports a flat nose. Both bullets have a long bore-riding section in front of the driving bands to assist in proper alignment with the bore.

One of the best loads I've used with either of these two bullets is 19.0 grains of SR-4759. With this load and a bullet having a hardness of about 11 or 12 BHN, one can easily shoot all day and stay well within the two-inch mark. Although I never chronographed that particular load, 15 grains of SR-4759 behind the RCBS bullet gave an average velocity of 1,310 fps with a velocity spread of 26 fps.

A charge of 18.0 grains of 4227 works about at well as the 4759. For the lighter loads, 10.0 grains of Unique works well with just about any bullet from 115 to 180 grains.

Because I am so involved with the use of cast bullets and paper patched bullets in the .45-70, I never really spent the time on the .30-40 that the cartridge deserves. However, after seeing how well paper patched bullets worked in the larger bore, I was determined to do some experimenting with paper patched bullets in the .30-40.

Using my RCBS mould, I cast some bullets of my regular alloy (a Duke's mixture) having a hardness of 11 or 12 BHN, as well as some of pure lead. These bullets were then wiped with CSL-71 case sizing lube from Rooster Laboratories and pushed through a SAECO .309-inch sizing die. The lube was wiped off and the bullets patched with nine-pound onionskin, bringing them up to a diameter of .316 inch.

In front of 19.0 grains of SR-4759, these bullets shot the same as their grooved counterpart, but loaded in front of 32.0 grains of IMR-4064, the story was different. Cases for the hard bullets (11 to 12 BHN) had been full-length resized, whereas those for the pure lead bullets were left unsized and the bullets finger-seated in the cases.

When clocked across the Oehler chronograph, the hard bullets gave an average velocity of 1,932 fps with an extreme spread of 27 fps, while the pure lead bullets from the same mould and using the same charge of powder gave an average velocity of 1,751 fps with an extreme spread of 74 fps!

Although it would take a number of tests to determine what caused the vast difference in velocity — case sizing or bullet hardness, or possibly both — one thing is apparent: If a man is really serious about his shooting, and is interested in working up good loads, he needs a chronograph. It took me many years to learn this, but the evidence is irrefutable. For years my position was that velocity was secondary; the important thing was what happened out on the target. That remains true today — I'll take accuracy anytime in preference to velocity. Accuracy at any velocity, however, is closely linked with velocity spread — the difference in the high and low velocity of a specified number of shots — and the only way one can know the velocity spread is to use a chronograph.

I should take this one step further and say that velocity spread is closely linked to ignition, and that sometimes a wide velocity spread is corrected by slightly increasing the charge or possibly going to a faster-burning powder in order to get better ignition.

Although I found it was a relatively simple matter to paper patch practically any grooved bullet from a standard mould, I much prefer a smooth-sided, cupped-base, flat-nosed bullet cast especially for that purpose. Charlie Canoll made such a mould for me, casting a bullet with unpatched diameter of .302 inch and capable of weighing up to 220 grains. It's another project for the future, but based on what Charlie has been able to do in his Remington 788 .30-30, I'm fairly certain that before too many more months have passed, I'll be firing soft alloy 220-grain bullets from my Ruger No. 3 .30-40.

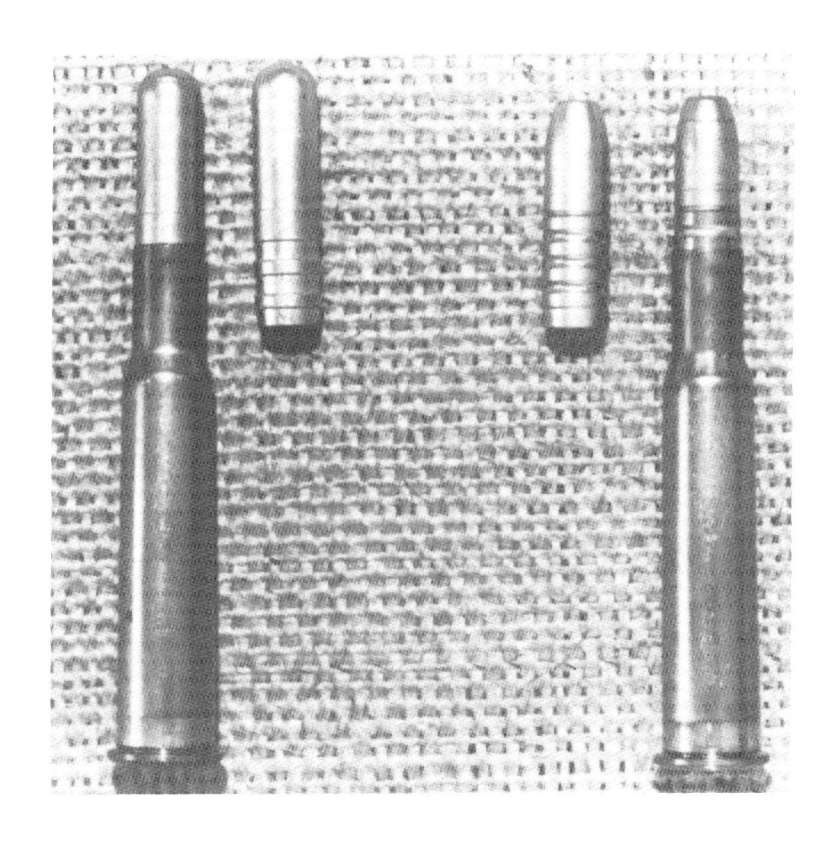

Left, a .30-40 Krag cartridge with a 220-grain cast bullet from a mould cut by Charlie Canoll. Right, the RCBS 30-180-FN bullet.

Cartridges loaded for use in Ruger single shots having freebored chambers. Note how the bullets are seated out just shy of the rifling. This produces better accuracy and provides greater case capacity if you so desire.

7

The .30-06

Colonel Townsend Whelen once wrote that the .30-06 is never a mistake. He was right. The .30-06 is, was and always will be a superb cartridge for just about anything you want to do with it. If the '06 has any fault, it is in the fact that a number of hunters, myself included, have at some time used the wrong bullet for the job at hand and blamed their subsequent failure on the cartridge instead of their own lack of knowledge at the time of the event. As I mentioned in the chapter covering the .300 Savage, I believe that when velocity exceeds 2,500 fps, the requirements of bullet structure relative to killing power become more stringent and less flexible. Back in 1949 such a thought had never occurred to me, or if it had, it was at the elementary level.

I got my first .30-06, a Winchester Model 70 serial number 89,722 on May 7, 1949. Even before I took it out of the store, I had a Lyman 48WJS aperture sight mounted on the receiver. This is one of the finest adjustable iron sights ever produced, and it is a shame that the shooting fraternity has become so infatuated with the scope that such sights as the Lyman 48 are now a thing of the past.

For weeks before I was able to bring that rifle home, I scrounged .30-06 cases wherever I could find them. In those days handloaders were regarded as something between the court jester and the Wizard of Oz, a person who you sat back and secretly admired, but who you shied away from for fear of catching whatever it was he had.

From the time my brother Wilfrid traded his .32 Special for the 1917 Enfield .30-06, he fired at least a box of factory ammunition into the old chestnut stump out behind the barn every week. Not wanting to contaminate the insides of his rifle with such wizardry as reloaded ammunition, his expended cases lay there in the pasture, hidden in the grass where they landed after being ejected from his rifle.

I spent hours out there toeing the grass looking for those precious cases, then took them home and ran them through a Lyman vise-type resizing die. I didn't know much about case-sizing lube at that time, but as I recall I used a mixture of kerosene and graphite. Although it worked, such a concoction is not recommended at a time when there are dozens of good case-sizing lubes on the market. During the years since, I've used everything from Crisco™ to waterpump grease to STP™, all of which worked better than the kerosene and graphite.

As mentioned earlier, I was out of a job at that time, but with the help and understanding of a good wife, even before I had my new rifle, I had purchased a Lyman 310 nutcracker tool for reloading .30-06 cartridges. Then came the primers, the powder and the bullets.

Our thinking process changes with knowledge. In those days Hercules Hi-Vel No. 2 was a very popular powder and it was the first powder I ever purchased, but for some reason I didn't like the way it performed. On Charlie Canoll's recommendation, I switched to IMR-3031. I even gave Charlie the remainder of that can of Hi-Vel No. 2 because I was afraid of having two different kinds of powder in the house at the same time — a short-lived philosophy. For a load I settled upon 43.0 grains of IMR-3031 behind the Speer 180-grain bullet. Today I would certainly go to a much slower burning powder like IMR-4350, for that weight bullet, but in those days economy came first and I could get more loads per pound from the IMR-3031 than from IMR-4350.

After shooting the '06 a few times, I graduated from leaning against the apple tree to taking a prone position with a tight sling. It was then that I discovered that the bead front sight left a lot to be desired. It covered too much of the target for fine shooting, and I didn't like the idea of a six o'clock hold because I had never been able to figure out just where six o'clock was on a woodchuck, crow or deer.

Deciding that I wanted a crosshair front sight, I set about designing one. It used a steel tube $\frac{3}{8}$-inch long with an outside diameter of $\frac{15}{32}$ inch and an inside diameter of $\frac{9}{32}$ inch silver-soldered to a standard $\frac{3}{8}$-inch dovetail base .150-inch thick. For crosshairs, I took a card of sewing needles and, holding each needle at arm's length, I selected the finest needle I could see with sharp definition. It was .023-inch diameter.

Charlie Canoll made the sight for me and blued it, and it stayed on that rifle for as long as I owned it. It was not the best sight for a target having a solid black bullseye, because the crosshairs blended in with the bull, but the sight was superb on game.

I recall that once Ernie and I were sitting near the top of a sidehill watching the fields below for chucks when I spied one standing in tall grass a full 250 yards away. Of course, at that range, the vertical hair in the front sight more than covered the chuck, but by aligning the sights off to one side of the chuck with the horizontal hair sitting on his head, and then moving the rifle to the left until the vertical hair covered the chuck, I made a center hit in the chest. In fact, I made a lot of good shots with that rifle and sight combination.

Using the .30-06 brought me face-to-face with the realities of shooting economics. With powder at $1.75 per pound and .30-caliber bullets at a similar low price, it was obvious that loading my own ammunition was far more economical than the store-bought stuff. It also became apparent that because of this difference in cost, I was doing a lot more shooting than ever before, and that it was just whetting my appetite to do even more. Compounding the situation was the fact that we lived out in the country in an old sidehill farmhouse sans running water and inside facilities, and that being out of work gave me time to do more shooting than usual. In fact, the echoes of my shots could be heard almost daily.

The reality was that if I was going to do all this shooting, I had to find a more economical source of bullets. I purchased a few boxes of .30-caliber M2 bullets from the DCM, and although these would zip through a 12-inch hickory with no problem, they weren't good for anything except target work. I wanted a bullet I could use for almost anything I wanted to shoot at. It was at that time I started looking for a bullet I could make at home which would be accurate and deliver reliable expansion on game. It was a search that took me over 30 years to complete.

The first step in the right direction was a visit to Charlie's gunshop at Waverly, New York. Charlie explained the use of cast bullets, the difference between a plain-base bullet and a gas-checked bullet, and the occasional advantages of the Ideal No. 308241 154-grain plain-base .30-30 bullet over the squatty 115-grain Ideal No. 3118 for the .32-20. I couldn't get it through my head at that time that because of the longer bearing surface on the former, I could drive it just as fast or faster than the .32-20 bullet, and with better accuracy.

I went home that day with Charlie's Ideal 3118 mould and visions of all sorts of containers filled with bullets.

Few people talked about hard bullets at that time. They were used by the more experimental-minded, but for the average handloader and shooter, if he was bent at all in the direction of cast bullets for rifles, it was usually a relatively soft lead-tin alloy of about 16 to 1. An alloy of 10 to 1 was considered hard.

I had already accumulated both lead and tin, and from the backyard I had dug up an old cast iron pot about six inches deep and 10 inches across. Sometime during the age of antiquity, the kettle had acquired a crack and a blacksmith had closed it by making a circular strap like a barrel hoop and driving it on. With the find of that kettle, cracked or not, I had a melting pot. I borrowed one of my wife's old teaspoons from the cupboard drawer and formed a pouring spout by catching the end of the spoon between vise jaws and squeezing.

For a heat source, I used the three-burner kerosene stove we had in the kitchen, but in order to get things hot enough to melt that kettle of lead, I had to turn the flame up so that it licked at the bottom of the kettle. That was bad enough, but after I had the metal melted, I was in unknown territory and had to rely solely on what I had read, e.g., that after you melted the metal, you had to flux it by stirring in a chunk of beeswax about the size of a walnut.

Now there are big walnuts and there are small walnuts. I'm not certain how much difference it would have made, but I chose the big one and dropped in a matching chunk of beeswax. The smoke rolled. Little black things that you couldn't catch between a thumb and forefinger floated in the air. Clean starched curtains that hung on every window grew limp and sooty. It was almost as though the kitchen had turned into a steam locomotive freight yard, and it was the first, last and only time I ever cast bullets in the kitchen.

With the damage done, however, I cast bullets at a pace that had to have broken all records. I have long forgotten whether the mould I used was an old solid iron affair or one of the newer ones with wooden handles, but regardless, it didn't take long to cast better than 400 of the little projectiles which I thought would last for a long time.

I was proud of those bullets. I thought I had done great for my first time at casting bullets. Then Charlie looked them over and in a manner in which only Charlie could say it, said "Well, if we sort them out, we might find fifteen or twenty we can use."

That was when I learned that casting bullets is an exercise in quality control and not unlimited production. If a cast bullet isn't perfect, chuck it back into the pot. Better yet, cast slowly and methodically until you get good bullets, and then keep repeating the same process over and over again.

After another casting session (in an old chicken coop, this time), I had some decent bullets. These were lubricated and then sized to .311 inch in my Lyman 310 nutcracker tool. They were loaded in front of 15½ grains of SR-4759.

For the job I wanted to do, there were far better powders to use, probably Unique or even Bullseye. I was quite velocity conscious at the time, however, and wanted every bit I could get out of that little bullet even though it wasn't intended for such extremes. Accuracy wasn't all that good even at squirrel hunting ranges, leading was a sometimes problem and, as I recall, the powder didn't burn all that clean. However, since I had sold my shotgun to help pay for the rifle, I used the '06 and the Ideal 3118 bullet for small game hunting that year. My records show that I shot 13 squirrels and one rabbit.

By the spring of 1950, I had followed Charlie's advice to a degree and switched to the 154-grain Ideal No. 308241 .30-30 bullet. Still trying to squeeze the last foot per second velocity from a plain-base bullet, I used a ⅛-inch cork wad under the bullet and increased the powder charge to 18.0 grains of SR-4759. I also concocted a lube which may have been way ahead of its time. It was a dip lube made by mixing Duco (DuPont) household cement with an equal part of acetone and adding ¼ spoonful of finely powdered graphite for each tube of cement. The bullets were sized first, then dipped in the lube up to the crimping groove and, before the bases dried, tamped base-down in powdered graphite. The cord wad also was used.

This treatment virtually put a jacket on the bullet. In fact, I recall throwing some of these bullets back in the pot and watching the bullets melt, leaving the Duco jacket intact. However, the Duco cement and graphite added diameter to the bullet and sometimes the lube was scraped off during the bullet seating process. It was an educational experiment toward my goal of a suitable homemade bullet, and it would take a heavier charge than the same bullet with a wax-graphite lube.

In April of 1950 I was called back to work and made the acquaintance of Jerry Biles. Jerry had a 1917 Enfield for which he reloaded, a Lyman No. 45 Lubricator and Sizer, and a Hensley & Gibbs double-cavity mould for casting a 170-grain, gas-checked bullet with a semi-spitzer point. It was shaped just about like the popular Lyman Ideal bullet No. 311413 weighing 169 grains. It was one of the few pointed bullets that gave good accuracy.

With Jerry, my bullet casting took on a whole new outlook. I purchased a gasoline plumber's furnace from Sears Roebuck, and with a melting pot provided by Jerry, we started working with hard alloys. Neither the term Linotype nor the product was familiar to either of us, but we had no problem getting all the lead, tin and antimony we wanted and it wasn't long before we were casting extremely hard bullets.

Velocity was still a prime factor in our reloading. Jerry used 35.0 grains of IMR-4320 in his Enfield and shot some excellent groups. I used 38.0 grains of the same powder and shot a number of gray squirrels with the Hensley & Gibbs bullet that fall. Looking back on it, that was an extremely dangerous thing to do as those hard bullets would ricochet off the ground or zing through a two-inch branch to pick off a squirrel on the backside. The load was far too powerful for use in the woods without a positive backstop. I should have stayed with the Ideal 3118 bullet or the gas-checked version Ideal 311316 and a few grains of Bullseye — just enough to get about 1,000 fps. Then I would have had a good squirrel load.

Still not realizing the important relation of bullet shape to cast bullets. I wanted a bullet a bit more streamlined than Jerry's Hensley & Gibbs. Thus, I ordered the Lyman Ideal No. 308329 with a fine hollowpoint. This was a spitzer-pointed bullet weighing 173 grains in a very hard alloy. It gave good accuracy, though I can't remember how it compared to the Hensley & Gibbs bullet, but it was far more streamlined and begged for higher velocity. In an effort to comply, I tried the new bullet with 55.0 to 57.0 grains of IMR-4350. Sometimes three shots out of a five-shot group would cluster together, but to get real accuracy I had to drop back to 35.0 grains of IMR-4320.

Accuracy or not, hard bullets at higher velocity are not dependable killers in the deer woods, and since that was my ultimate goal with a cast bullet, I turned in a different direction.

Since I was working nights on a turret lathe, I usually had the last one to 1½ hours of the shift to do what we termed "government jobs," something for Number One. In this capacity I often turned out hand-held bullet sizing dies of different diameters, or whatever else I could dream up including blank die sets which Charlie could later ream out with a chambering reamer.

With opportunities like this, it didn't take too long to come up with the idea of cutting $\frac{3}{32}$-inch driving bands from $\frac{5}{16}$-inch copper tubing. These little rings were then driven through a .310-inch die and placed in the bullet mould between the grease grooves. On the 308329 bullet, I used two of these driving bands and loaded the bullet in front of 56 grains of IMR-4350. While I don't recall what kind of grouping I got, nor did I include it in any of my notes, they apparently shot fairly well, because my next step was to try the same bullet with copper driving bands in a soft alloy.

Using a 10-to-1 lead-tin alloy, the No. 308329 bullet was 10 grains heavier, or 180 grains. A handful of these were loaded in front of 56.0 grains of IMR-4350 and taken to the pasture lot shooting range for testing.

I still can recall the peculiar sound that first shot made as I bellied down at 100 yards and touched one off. It wasn't quite like shooting inside a wooden barrel, and yet it had that same hollow reverberating characteristic. The target was unscathed, so I moved up to 50 yards and tried again. Once more a hollow-log boom and no hole in the target. Nor could I see a fresh hole in the old chestnut tree in the area around the target.

Off to my right about 40 yards away was a steep sidehill, and, I reasoned that if the target was shifted to the sidehill, then I could at least see where the bullets were hitting. I made the move. Once more I bellied down, took a good aim and squeezed off the shot.

Nothing. No hole in the target and no spurt of dust to indicate a hit. Three or four more shots were cranked through with the same result, and then it dawned on me that the bullets were so soft they were coming apart as soon as they left the muzzle. This was the first time I had ever considered the centrifugal force imposed on a bullet due to rifling twist and velocity. How much effect it has on the hunting bullet relative to killing power or wounding capacity is still up for grabs. However, since I've seen evidence of bullets continuing to rotate after all linear travel is finished, I believe the effects of centrifugal force relative to wound capability are significant although they may vary depending upon bullet structure. That is, with a given twist, a lightly constructed bullet is going to expand faster and farther than a more heavily constructed bullet.

If my successes with cast bullets weren't anything to rave about, neither was my success with the jacketed variety. Oh, I had good accuracy, but the .30-06 is a lot like a four-wheel-drive vehicle. Because it performs well where it is supposed to perform well, we expect it to perform well under situations for which it is not intended.

You must understand that back in 1949 and the early 1950s jacketed bullets had not reached the level of perfection they have today. There was considerable room for improvement and I must say that the various manufacturers were busy working toward those improvements. More than that, since handloading as we know it today was in its infancy, sporting goods stores didn't have a dozen shelves loaded down with various brands of different weights and caliber bullets. They might carry one brand in a few popular calibers and weights, but you had to place an order for the rest of them.

Thus it was that when I first started out with the '06, it was the readily available Speer 180-grain softpoint that I used. Although I had heard some criticism from a few locals that the bullets didn't always expand, I never had a problem with them. I shot several woodchucks with the heavy bullet that summer — woodchucks that my wife canned to help put us through the winter — and that fall I shot my deer with the same bullet backed by 43.0 grains of IMR-3031.

That large doe was taken at about 30 yards. The bullet struck about three inches behind the front leg halfway up the body. It blew the lungs apart, but was too far aft to touch the heart. The doe ran about 60 yards, making a semicircle that brought her back across a fire trail where I fired the second shot, breaking her front leg and striking her in the brisket. The second shot was unnecessary, although at the time I didn't know it.

In all probability had I stuck with the 180-grain bullet I would have stayed with the .30-06. The velocity craze, however, was just starting — at least that's the way it seemed to me — and the shooting and sporting magazines were full of articles expounding the efficiency of the .270 with its 130-grain bullet and the .30-06 with the 150-grain bullet. Jack O'Connor was one of the top writers of the time and his love for the .270 was widely known. In one article Jack had written, he stated that his choice .30-06 load for deer and antelope was the Remington 150-grain bronzepoint backed by 52.0 grains of IMR-4320. This was good enough for me and I ordered several of the Remington bullets from Charlie.

The Remington bronzepoint probably is one of the most beautiful bullets ever developed. It was streamlined and it never battered in the magazine. Coupled with the load of 52.0 grains of IMR-4320, it was superbly accurate and flat shooting, although when I first started using the bullet,

I used 44.0 grains of IMR-3031. In my records for 1950, it shows that on May 20 I shot a chuck with that load at a range of 80 yards. The bullet entered the left side of the chest and went out between the shoulder blades, but failed to expand. Immediately after this, I switched to the 52.0 grain load of IMR-4320 and had no further problems. In one case, on August 23 of that year, I shot a crow at 150 yards and the bullet apparently expanded well as it disemboweled the crow.

Still, there was an indication that on that one failure at the lower velocities the Remington bronzepoint might not perform as expected. However, the bullet was designed for deer, not woodchucks. Further, it was extremely accurate so I took it deer hunting.

The first deer I shot with that load was standing quietly in the middle of a field about 150 yards away. The bullet struck directly over the foreleg, smashed through the spine where it dipped down between the shoulder blades and made a two-inch exit hole on the opposite side. The deer dropped in its tracks and I was elated. Even today there is little doubt in my mind that if one is hunting deer or antelope in open country where he can pick a shot, he can do little better than use a good 150-grain bullet in the '06 backed with 52.0 grains of IMR-4320.

Open country shooting or sitting on a stump where I could thread a bullet between trees and bushes to pick off an unsuspecting deer some distance away has never been my way of hunting. I have always been a walker, prowling the brush lots and hemlock thickets. Oh yes, I've shot many a deer from a stump while sitting down to rest. Nowadays with everyone sitting on their tail on the opening day, it doesn't show good judgment to do a lot of walking lest you step into a set of crosshairs held by some guy perched high in a tree. Still, even today I don't do a lot of sitting, and after noon of the second day I'm on my feet most of the time.

Back in 1951 the average hunter had not yet acquired a scope, nor had he taken to the trees to do his hunting.

Like me, a lot of hunters poked the brush. For this game the 150-grain bullet in the '06 is not the bullet to use.

My first failure occurred in the forenoon. As usual I was poking around when a doe came charging out of nowhere and ripped past me not 40 feet away. The shot was a classic raking shot, behind the ribs at an angle that should take it forward through the lungs. Of course, it didn't. The doe never slowed, and despite a heavy blood trail at first, the blood soon petered out and the tracks became mixed with dozens of others. I never found her although I knew she couldn't live too long. I had placed the shot well, and if the deer had been standing unexcited, she might have dropped in her tracks.

Early that afternoon I had a second failure. Coming up over a low ridge, I saw my brother Allan and a guest hunter off to my left in the process of shooting at two doe running full-tilt through the timber. I picked out an opening far ahead of them and when the first deer crossed it, I fired. I saw the animal flinch and keep on going. When the second doe hit the clearing, I fired a second time and she piled up with a broken spine. Not knowing the extent of the wound at the time, and having already suffered enough failures, I fired two more shots to anchor her.

Allan, the guest and I all arrived at the downed deer at about the same time. One glance showed the tremendous devastation of the three bullets, and I wanted to get on the track of the first deer that had crossed the clearing. So turning to the guest, I said: "I believe you shot at that deer first."

He was a big man and without a moment's hesitation scooped the deer up in his arms without even taking the time to gut it out or tag it. As he headed off toward our woods headquarters, I started on the track of the first deer I had shot at.

It was the same story all over again, a heavy blood trail at first with the blood petering out as the wound closed over and her tracks blended in with others. I never found her.

Late that afternoon as I was working my way back to our headquarters, I spotted another doe standing in a little thicket 50 or 60 yards away. I put the crosshair front sight on her chest and squeezed off the shot. She ran.

I couldn't believe it. I knew I had made a good shot on the animal, but when I picked up her track, there was almost no blood at all. She fell only a short distance away. Upon dressing her out, I found that the 150-grain Remington bronzepoint had totally disintegrated within the chest cavity — which was filled with blood — and the little bronze tip of the bullet lay under the hide on the off-side.

Now for those who believe the theory that a bullet should completely disintegrate within the animal in order to dissipate all of its energy, I have but one question: If a bullet won't go through a deer crosswise, how in the world can you expect it to ever reach the chest cavity on a raking shot?

Had there not been snow on the ground, there is a good possibility I never would have found that deer — the third one of the day. With the entrance wound closed over and no exit wound, there would have been no blood trail. Despite the fact the deer didn't travel far after the shot, they don't always have to in order to lose themselves in the brush and leaves.

That was the last deer I ever shot at with the .30-06. I did return to the 180-grain bullet, but carried the '06 in the deer woods for only one day after that.

Again, I want to emphasize that there is nothing wrong with the .30-06. The error usually is on the part of the hunter, just as it was in my case. For the manner and terrain in which the 150-grain bullet was totally inadequate. Jack O'Connor may have found it to be a good bullet in the areas where he hunted and compatible with the method by which he hunted, but I don't know that Jack ever hunted in the Pennsylvania woodlots. Nor do I know the details of his particular method of hunting.

My experience with the Remington 150-grain bronze-point bullet illustrates only too well the critical importance of bullet structure in relation to velocity. As I had seen on the first chuck I shot with that bullet, at the lower velocities the bullet didn't always expand. Maybe it would have on deer, but I wouldn't bet on it. Certainly at the higher velocities it disintegrated with little chance for deep penetration.

However, I could easily have had the reverse problem if I had chosen the 180-grain bullet in the '06 — a problem of nonexpansion. For example, in my .32 Special and Dad's .300 Savage, he always used Silvertip bullets, the 170-grain in the .32 and the 180-grain bullet in the .300. These never failed to expand. I recall a number of instances, however, and I photographed some bullet wounds in deer, where a 180-grain Silvertip from a .30-06 bored through like a full jacket with no hint of expansion!

What this all boils down to is that when you get into muzzle velocities much over 2,500 fps, it becomes exceedingly difficult to design a bullet that will expand properly without breakup at any range and on any game, be it a 125-pound deer or a 900-pound elk. Below a muzzle velocity of 2,500 fps you can use a thin jacket and a pure lead core and be assured of positive expansion with little weight loss. Low weight loss usually means penetration good enough for a raking shot. I also must add that regardless of velocity, I always favor the heavier bullets for a given caliber.

The old Western Tool and Copper Works bullet was one of the finest I ever used. The jacket on this bullet was made of tubing, though not a pure copper tubing as in the Barnes bullets. To the best of my knowledge, .30-caliber WTCW bullets were offered in only two weights, 150 and 172 grains. They both had a fine hollow point which I always understood, but I don't know for certain if it was drilled. Both bullets were quite accurate, but considerably different in structure.

I used a lot of the WTCW 150-grain bullets on woodchucks and crows, and in every instance the bullet expanded violently. The 172-grain bullet, however, was far more rugged. Charlie Canoll tried them on deer and found that they often failed to expand. Conversely, Hosea Sarber, a well-known Alaskan game warden at that time who wrote several fine articles for the *American Rifleman*, used the 172-grain WTCW bullet backed by 48.0 grains of IMR-4320 on the big brownies and considered the bullet almost perfect for the job. Coming from a man who had shot a number of the big bears, we have to listen. Once again, however, this points out the importance of matching bullet structure with the velocity of the cartridge and the game upon which it is to be used.

During the four years I used that Model 70 .30-06, I put better than 6,000 rounds through the barrel. Had it not been for the bad experience with the 150-grain Remington bronzepoints, I might still have that rifle today. As it was, sometime during the latter part of July 1953, I took the old '06 to town and traded it in on a new Winchester Model 70 chambered for the .375 H&H Magnum.

My shooting family circa 1950. Betty is holding her Arisaka 6.5x.257, Dawn has her double-barreled popgun and I have my Winchester Model 70 .30-06. At four years of age, Dawn went hunting with me many times.

8

The .375 H&H Magnum

It was exactly 4:30 P.M. Winter evening gloom had already set in and darkness was only minutes away. The air was thick with snow, so thick that the buck was almost on the perimeter of vision. One doe had already crossed the trail and stopped, her head twisted over her shoulder, while a second doe stood in the middle of the trail looking straight at me.

I could see only the buck's head and part of his neck, the rest of his body was a dim, broken outline obscured by a thicket of briars which separated us. It was now or never. I had trailed the group of deer for over 1½ hours and as I stood there, I wondered at my chances of putting a bullet through the intervening brush. Certainly my .30-06 wouldn't have done it, but could the .375 H&H?

The Ruger No. 1 found my shoulder and, as the safety snickered forward, I nestled the bead of the front sight into the U-notch of the rear, aligned them on the spot where I thought the buck's chest should be and pressed the trigger. A lance of flame bit a chunk from the gloom as the buck collapsed, done in by a 300-grain Hornady round-nose, softpoint bullet which plowed through 40 feet of briars to strike the buck exactly where I wanted. That's the way I like a rifle to perform!

Many times I have written that the .375 H&H Magnum was the greatest cartridge to ever come across a drawing board. After more than 35 years' association with this fine cartridge in several different rifles and with thousands of rounds fired downrange, I have yet to discover any single factor that would change that opinion. With a trajectory as flat as the .30-06 — yes, a trajectory out to 300 yards so close to the .338 that no hunter could tell the difference — and more poop when it gets there, the .375 H&H surely is as close to the mythical all-around rifle as one will ever get.

I am not the only man to make that claim. Far better men than myself with far greater experience have used the .375 H&H on everything from the smallest of the African plains game to the elephant, rhino and Cape buffalo. On the other end of the scale, for 23 years I used this fine cartridge on everything from blackbirds to feral dogs to woodchucks to deer. The .375 H&H with the proper bullet is the finest, most reliable deer cartridge I've ever used.

Since some may question my comparison of the .375 H&H with the .338, take a look at the paper ballistics of bullets with comparable sectional density and ballistic shape at the nominal muzzle velocity for which the cartridge is listed. Using a 200-yard sight setting, a 300-grain Hornady .375 bullet at 2,500 fps drops 13 inches at 300 yards, while the 250-grain roundnose Hornady .338 bullet at 2,600 fps drops 11½ inches — a 1½-inch difference — with a slight energy advantage for the .375.

Comparing the 270-grain Spire Point .375 projectile at 2,700 fps against the 225-grain Spire Point .338 at 2,800 fps, both bullets have virtually the same drop at 300 yards with about 375 foot-pounds of energy difference in favor of the .375 H&H. In both cases, the .375 has a significant advantage in weight, which adds up to deeper penetration with all other things being equal.

While the .338 Winchester Magnum is a superb cartridge (far better I believe than the .300 Winchester or the 7mm Remington Magnum), the facts are that you can't put 10 pounds of sugar in a five-pound bag. The shorter .338 case just doesn't hold as much fuel as the .375 H&H. Of course, that is not all bad if you subscribe to my previously stated theory about adding bullet weight and/or diameter at velocities over 2,500 fps to obtain greater killing power.

At any rate, I began thinking in terms of the .375 H&H early in 1952, before the .338 was a twinkle in Winchester's eye. By that time it had become apparent to me that my method of deer hunting demanded a cartridge that embodied the best characteristics of both the .30-06 and the .45-70 — flat cross-field trajectory as well as up-close, thick-brush shots at the south end of a buck headed north. Unlike most hunters who choose to spend hours on a stand, I always liked to walk, prowling the brush lots and sometimes skirting the edge of a field as I moved from one brush lot or woods to another.

I had considerable reservations about the .375. I weighed 125 pounds at the time and didn't know whether or not I could handle the recoil. At that time Elmer Keith was the only gun writer who downplayed the big rifle's recoil, equating it with that of a 12-gauge shotgun with high-brass loads, whereas most other writers emphasized the brutal recoil of the .375 H&H as compared to the '06, .270 or .257 Roberts. It was enough to scare a man half to death.

During the summer of 1952 I made the plunge and traded my older brother Wilfrid out of an Eddystone 1917 Enfield having a perfect five-land barrel. That fall I took the Enfield and $50 to Charlie Canoll to have it rebarreled and chambered for the .375 H&H. It was a decision I never regretted.

The new barrel was a Douglas, finishing off at 26 inches long with a perfectly straight taper from the breech to a 7/8-inch muzzle. This made quite a heavy rifle weighing in at 11 pounds, 9 ounces when equipped with a sling and a Weaver KV scope that I had recently purchased. For the wood, I took the original stock, spliced on a couple of pieces of oak to raise the comb, and added a recoil pad. Being a butcher of wood, the results were functional but far from pretty. In fact, the stock was downright homely.

But talk about accuracy! That old blunderbuss would shoot like there was no tomorrow! Neither Charlie nor I had ever fired anything as rambunctious as the .375 H&H, yet when we took it out for the first time on a bitter cold day in January 1953, that gun showed us the inherent accuracy of the .375 H&H.

The load we used, one which I continued to use for years, was 76.0 grains of IMR-4350 behind a 300-grain Barnes bullet. After one or two shots to see that the rifle was going to stay in one piece, and then two or three sighters, we fired a five-shot group, calling one shot out as it was fired. Even including the shot that was called out, the group still measured ⅝ x 1⅛ inches. Had the shot not been tossed, the group would have been well under one inch. This was at 90 yards as we were testing the rifle in a local gravel pit and that was the maximum range we could get.

The big rifle proved exceedingly accurate. Early that spring I measured off 400 yards behind the barn and measured from a prone position fired five shots that measured four inches horizontally by 6¾ inches vertically.

Knowing that I wanted to do a lot of shooting with the .375, and that the cost of jacketed bullets in the quantity I had in mind would soon send us to the poorhouse, I ordered a mould from Lyman for bullet No. 375449. This is a gas-checked bullet weighing from 260 to 278 grains on the alloy used. It had been highly recommended by Elmer Keith.

In those days I wasn't all that fussy about how hard or soft my cast bullets were. Chunks of lead and lead alloy were thrown into the pot, fluxed liberally with a large chunk of paraffin and then cast into bullets. The bullets usually were lubricated by the old Kake Kutter pie pan method with a home-brewed concoction that was equally as haphazard as the bullet alloy. Yet, somehow it all came together, and when the bullets were loaded over 44.0 grains of IMR-3031 or 47.0 grains of government surplus 4895, they shot where the rifle was looking and wreaked havoc on whatever was on the far end. The load afforded me a lot of economical shooting and taught me a few things about primers and ignition.

One Sunday I had invited Albert M. Armstrong, an old Pennsylvania market hunter, for dinner — the noon meal in those days. After dinner was finished, we went out on the front porch where my portable benchrest stood — I was just beginning to use a benchrest — and started shooting. It so happened that when I loaded the ammunition for that day's exercise, I loaded about half of it using Winchester 120 primers and finished up with Federal 210 primers because I had run out of the 120s.

I was doing the shooting when the switch in ammunition was made. Immediately I thought I could hear the firing pin "click" on the primer before the rifle fired. After firing several rounds this way, I turned to Bert and asked him if I was hearing things, but the Old Man had been down that road before and knew without my telling what the problem was and what had caused it. From that day to this, whenever using that load in the .375 H&H, I've always filled the air space in the case with a slightly compressed measure of Cream of Wheat. In the .375 H&H, the Cream of Wheat has worked better than anything else I ever tried, though I suspect today's Super Grex shot buffer would be equally as good, or maybe even better.

My gas check load from that rifle would always stay inside two inches at 100 yards, and would drop 10 inches at 200 yards. One Sunday that spring I was visiting a friend. Since it was raining, we were laying in a haymow shooting through an open window across a swamp at rocks on a sidehill. The swamp was alive with blackbirds, and pretty soon one of the red-winged variety landed in the very tip-top of a willow. Sam asked me to adjust the sights on the rifle so that he could hit that particular bird with one of the cast bullets. I did and he did. The range was about 150 yards, but when Sam pressed the trigger, the bird exploded in a puff of feathers.

Sometime about July 1953, a young doctor came to the house one day asking if I would sight in a rifle for him.

He was going to Africa as a missionary doctor, and was taking along a Winchester Model 70 .375 H&H.

Never in my life had I been so impressed with a single firearm. Harry had had the barrel cut off just behind the front sight ramp, and a new ramp installed. He had also had a scope mounted in a Williams' offset mount, and wanted me to sight the rifle in using both the scope and the folding leaf iron sights on the barrel.

The rifle handled like a dream. It was short, handy and pointed where you were looking. Far lighter than my Enfield, when I threw it to my shoulder the first time, I knew I had to have one like it.

Shooting the doctor's rifle was an education in itself. I sighted in at 100 yards from a prone position so that when the crosshairs quartered the bull, the bullets struck about two inches high. When I was satisfied with the scope, I started in with the iron sights.

Now, I don't know about other men, but when I use iron sights my head is lower than with a scope and I have a tendency to crawl a stock. That is, I get just a bit closer to the sights. With Harry's rifle, I fired only one shot using the iron sights and had a deep, cookie-cutter gash over my right eyebrow. The blood streamed down my face as I handed the rifle back to him stating with no uncertain degree of emphasis that I would not shoot it again until he had replaced the Williams offset mount with a Weaver top-detachable mount so that the scope could be removed before using the iron sights. A week later Harry was back with the new mounts installed, and we sighted the rifle in as he wanted.

Ever since I bought that first Weaver KV scope back in 1952, I've never carried a rifle in the woods that didn't have a set of iron sights sighted in with the ammunition I was using. Nor have I ever attempted to use a set of iron sights with a scope mounted on the rifle.

On the day that I shot the buck mentioned at the beginning of this chapter, I had left the house at noon under a bright December sun carrying my Ruger No. 1 .375 H&H equipped with a Weaver K4 scope. Fifteen minutes later the snow started to dribble down, and by 2:30 P.M. it was snowing so hard that an exposed scope lens was covered in seconds. That was when I removed the scope, hung it from a loop around my neck and tucked it under my coat. Then I flipped up the rear iron sight and switched my ammunition from the Spire Point 270-grain Hornady to a 300-grain Hornady roundnose bullet. I was just 27 paces from that buck when I fired, but without the use of iron sights, an aimed shot would have been impossible.

Since that day back in 1953 when I sighted in Harry Zimmer's rifle, I have removed and replaced scopes in the field dozens of times because of bad weather. I have always carried a handmade key or wrench to fit the mounting clamp nuts, and when replacing the scope I always tighten the nuts as tightly as possible with this particular key. By doing it this way, the scope always returns to the same place each time and I never have to worry about a shift in point of impact.

Two or three days after sighting in Harry's rifle, I took my Winchester Model 70 .30-06 to town and swapped it in on a new Model 70 .375 H&H.

The Winchester at that time had a 25-inch barrel. I used it for a few days and then took it to Charlie's gunshop and sawed the barrel off just behind the ramp, so that after crowning, the barrel length was 21¾ inches. It was absolutely perfect for carrying and woods handling. Charlie installed a new ramp of the proper height and the original front sight was fitted into the slot. With sling and scope, the rifle weighed 9¼ pounds.

Knowing that I was going to use the .375 that fall for deer hunting, I started looking around for a good deer bullet. The 300-grain Barnes bullet had a pretty rugged copper tubing jacket with only a small amount of lead exposed, and it didn't appear as though it would expand very much, if at all, on deer. As far as cast bullets were concerned, I had not yet reached the point where I felt I could rely on them for deer hunting, although I'm certain they would have worked just fine.

Charlie started the ball rolling by giving me some Winchester full-jacketed 255-grain .38-55 bullets, and I ordered 100 of the Remington softnose 255-grain bullets.

The full jackets were a surprise. Loading some of them in front of 68.0 grains of IMR-4064, they blew up like bombs on an old rotten log that lay some distance from the house. They may have been full-jacketed, but the jacket was thin, intended for the black powder velocity of the old .38-55. I have no idea just how fast I was driving them, but my guess is that they were whizzing along at about 2,500 fps.

When I saw how the full-jacketed bullets behaved, I loaded up a few softpoints and went woodchuck hunting. I shot my first chuck with that load through the paunch at 187 paces. It nearly cut the chuck in two, but I knew I had the bullet and load I wanted to use for deer that fall.

I spotted the deer working its way through the beeches and hardwoods from quite a ways off. By the time it had crossed a couple of clearings, I knew it was a spike buck. To this day I remember judging the range to be about 100 yards when the buck reached the point at which I put the crosshairs directly over the foreleg and halfway up the body and pressed the trigger. He crumpled on the spot without so much as a kick of the hind leg.

Walking over to him, I counted the paces, all 57 of them, once more confirming the fact that guessed-at ranges usually are a lot longer than the measured variety. An autopsy on the buck showed the near shoulder was broken, the lungs pulped and the large arteries severed from the heart. Two ribs on each side were smashed and the meat was filled with small lumps of bullet core, jacket and bone splinters. One piece of flattened lead the size of a nickel had gone through the hide on the off-side as had another piece of about .30-caliber size. The meat was not bloodshot to any great extent, whereas a similar shot from an

'06 or .45-70 would have meant the loss of nearly all of the off-shoulder.

On that little buck, the .375 H&H exhibited two characteristics that I found true on almost every deer I ever shot with that cartridge. First, although the .375 always made a good-sized wound channel, it never bloodshot the meat to any great extent. I cannot even guess why this is true. As stated earlier, both the '06 and .45-70 with jacketed bullets are bad offenders in this respect, although I have recently found that soft paper-patched bullets in the .45-70 cause little bloodshot meat despite a large wound.

The second characteristic of the .375 H&H is that I never had but one deer move off after being smacked by one of those big bullets. Every deer but one dropped in its tracks. Even the one that didn't drop didn't move very far.

It was the first morning of deer season in 1958 and my wife and I were headed toward the top of the mountain, following an old dirt road. Within probably a quarter of a mile of the top, I looked uphill off to my right and there was a beautiful eight-point buck nibbling alfalfa or clover out in the middle of a field. We stood there and watched him for three or four minutes, and finally Betty said, "If you want that deer, you had better take it soon."

She was carrying the .45-70 that day, so I stepped off the road, crawled to the top of the bank and made the shot. The buck walked eight or 10 steps and stood there looking at me. I couldn't believe I had missed and I didn't want to take another shot, so I waited for him to drop. When he failed to do that, I poked him again over the foreleg and he dropped like a ton of brick.

For some reason — maybe I hit a piece of brush close to the muzzle or possibly a poor aim — my first bullet struck too far back and went through the paunch. Even at that, however, the buck was too sick to go anywhere.

Once again this illustrates the importance of balancing bullet structure with velocity and the type of game being hunted. Every bullet I ever used for deer in the .375 H&H

was designed for or modified to give rapid expansion. Since I felt that the .38-55 bullet used on the first buck was entirely too fragile for a raking shot, I took a second look at the big 300-grain Barnes bullets. As received from Barnes, they were made for deep penetration on heavy game. In fact, we butchered a beef cow on New Year's Day in 1954 and I found that I could drive one of the Barnes bullets lengthwise of the head with little expansion, but hollowpointing the same bullet with a $\frac{1}{8}$-inch center drill deeply enough to remove all of the exposed lead and put a slight bevel on the mouth of the cavity changed the entire picture.

Hollowpointing reduced the weight of the Barnes bullet to 285 grains, but it made them expand rapidly enough to do the job on light-framed animals such as deer. It was a hollowpointed Barnes bullet backed by 76 grains of IMR-4350 that I used to take the buck in 1958.

Sometime in the early 1960s I switched bullets again, this time going to a Hornady 270-grain roundnose bullet. Now if there is a better deer bullet than this one for the .375 H&H, I haven't met it. The jackets on these bullets didn't taper from a thick base to a thin nose, but were thinned down immediately ahead of the cannelure to about half the thickness of the base jacket. This, coupled with a generous amount of lead exposure, guarantees rapid expansion.

A deer's neck isn't much more than four to six inches thick if it's that much. Yet I made four neck shots with the Hornady bullet, and each of them gave ample expansion on just that small bit of flesh and bone. Needless to say, such a shot from the .375 H&H is virtually instant death.

Probably the best shot I ever made in my life was a neck shot on a doe about 1969. There was about six inches of snow on the ground and walking was difficult. However, I had seen a number of fresh deer tracks in the area and I knew that if I kept poking around sooner or later I would come eyeball-to-eyeball with a doe.

Well, it didn't happen quite that way. As I was working along the edge of an old slashing, I spotted four or five doe far below running uphill toward me. Just as I kicked the safety off and leaned against a tree for support, they all stopped, then wheeled and ran back down the hill. All except one. She stood back end to me, with her head raised high watching the others go.

As I said, a deer's neck isn't very thick, and the range was about 135 yards, but I put the crosshairs on her neck just below the head and pressed the trigger. When the rifle settled from recoil, there was a thin brown line showing above the snow, and I knew I had made the shot! The bullet struck dead center and that doe never knew what hit her.

To further illustrate the importance of using the proper bullet, the doctor I mentioned earlier hunted deer in 1953 using Winchester .375 H&H which I had sighted in for him. As I recall, Harry had never hunted deer before and didn't know their reaction or sometimes lack of reaction to being hit. Since Harry didn't know the country, his companions put him on the edge of a field bordered by woods.

Sometime during the forenoon, Harry looked up to see a fine buck going full tilt across the field and fed him two rounds from the .375 H&H. The buck kept on going, disappearing into the woods, and Harry chalked it up to a miss. Half an hour later, the same thing happened again, and again Harry figured he had missed.

About this time, one of Harry's companions, a dentist who was an experienced deer hunter, checked in on Harry to see what all the shooting was about. After Harry explained things to him, the two of them started checking the woods where the deer had disappeared. Sure enough, there were the two bucks, both shot twice through the chest *but with bullets that didn't open fast enough if they opened at all!* I don't know what bullet or ammunition Harry was using that day, but it wasn't satisfactory for deer, and without the help of a more experienced hunter, two fine bucks would have been wasted.

My Winchester Model 70 .375 H&H proved every bit as accurate as the Douglas-barreled Enfield. It was probably the most consistently accurate production rifle I ever owned. It was so accurate it helped me make such shots as hitting the doe in the back of the neck. An inch and a half on either side, and that doe would have been home free.

Like the .270 and a few other cartridges, the .375 H&H has an inherent accuracy that defies explanation other than to say it is well-balanced regarding case capacity, bullet weight and velocity. From a prone position and using the Barnes hollowpointed bullet I once placed 10 consecutive shots into ⅞-inch at 100 yards. The rifle would shoot as close as I could hold, which is to say that the capability of the rifle was better than my own.

For the type of hunting I do, I have always favored a roundnose bullet. I realize some experts claim that the roundnose bullet is as obsolete as the Model T Ford, but if we face facts, one doesn't realize any practical advantage in trajectory by using a pointed bullet until you get out to at least 150 yards. Conversely, the round nose provides for more reliable expansion because it has more lead exposure and because of the jacket's contour. The sides are closer to being parallel and, as such, are easier to spread apart than the closed-in form of the Spire Point.

However, where a Spire Point is needed, there is no substitute. In the middle of the first week of deer season in 1966, I stepped out of a thick brush lot, over a barbed wire fence and into a long 60-acre field that stretched uphill from me. To my immediate left, perhaps 40 feet away, was a hedgerow. As I looked up the hill, a huge buck came through the hedge and started downhill toward me.

As far away as he was, I could see his rack. It was tremendous — a rack like I had never seen before. Then I made the mistake of raising the rifle, and apparently a flash of sunlight off the barrel or scope lens spooked the buck so that he turned at right angles to run across the field just below the rim of the hill.

I was standing in a boggy area at the time, but bog or not, I sat down on the soggy ground, shoved my arm through the sling and squeezed off a shot. The crosshairs were held a couple feet ahead of the buck's nose and a foot or so above the backline, but through the scope I saw the bullet hit a few feet behind the deer down by his feet. I fired three shots as that buck went across the field and never touched a hair.

Later I wrote to Joyce Hornady, told him of my experience and suggested a 270-grain Spire Point for such occasions. His reply stated that the sales of .375 bullets were so minuscule that he couldn't justify both a roundnose and a Spire Point of the same weight. He went on to say, however, that if he received a sufficient number of requests, he would switch over to the Spire Point design.

A few years later the Spire Points were available and the difference in drop at 500 yards with a 200-yard sight setting is over 20 inches in favor of the Spire Point. That may not have been enough to make the difference for me on the big buck, but it is a significant advantage on long-range, open-country shooting.

Unfortunately, the Hornady 270-grain Spire Point had to be seated so deeply in the case to accommodate the magazine, that it had to "jump" too far before engaging the rifling. Thus, it did not deliver the accuracy in the Winchester that I had had with the roundnose bullets. However, the Spire Points were right at home in my Ruger No. 1 where the bullets could be seated out just shy of the rifling, and they performed well on deer.

In all honesty, I must say that by the time the 270-grain Spire Point came on the market, the accuracy from my Winchester had begun to deteriorate. The rifle had had at least 6,000 rounds through it, and I began looking for another rifle.

I got my first Ruger No. 1 single shot, the Tropical Model .375 H&H in October 1971. It was about the same overall length as the Winchester, a shade lighter, and much better handling because of the smaller grip and the somewhat shorter buttstock. In fact, the Ruger handled and pointed far better then the Winchester, but getting the Ruger to shoot was an education all by itself.

Using my standard load of 70.0 grains of IMR-4350 behind a 270-grain roundnose Hornady, I had difficulty keeping inside a four-inch group. Then noticing the freebore ahead of the chamber, I loaded up five more rounds with the bullets seated out just shy of the rifling. At 100 yards using a Weaver K6 scope, the five shots could barely be covered with a dinner plate.

To make a long story short, I put 2,200 rounds through that rifle during the next 10 months before I learned how to make it shoot. In the case of my No. 1 Tropical .375 H&H, it meant that I had to use a powder that ignited easily or, if a slow-burning powder was used, I had to load it full throttle.

I stumbled onto the truth of the matter one day when I loaded a few cartridges with the 300-grain Hornady bullet backed by 69.0 grains of IMR-4064. This load shot well, though not quite as well as in the Winchester. Had I used about 71.0 or 72.0 grains of the same powder behind the 270-grain bullet, I probably would have ended my problems right then. Instead, I went to 65.0 grains of IMR-3031 and again got good accuracy, though not quite as good as I had had from the Winchester. Later I went to 82.0 grains of the original H-4831 behind the 270-grain Spire Point and then the rifle shot as close as I could hold it.

All this goes to prove that each rifle is an individual and must be loaded for on that basis if one is to get the most out of a rifle. The single shots seem to be more individualistic than the bolt actions, especially if they are freebored ahead of the chamber.

I carried the .375 H&H for deer for the last time on the opening day of doe season in 1975, and on that date had an opportunity to try an endwise shot using the Hornady 270-grain Spire Point. The bullet struck on the left side of the neck just ahead of where the neck joins the body, traveling diagonally through the body to come to rest under the hide on the backside of the right hind leg. The retrieved bullet weighed 212 grains and measured ¾-inch across its widest part, making an almost perfect mushroom.

Despite the fact that over the years a number of experts have been critical of my use of the .375 H&H on deer (one of them going so far as to say that the two of them shouldn't be mentioned in the same article), it is difficult to argue with success. Granted, the cartridge is far more powerful than necessary to kill a deer, but if we had stopped at the first cartridge capable of killing a deer, we would still be using the .22 Short.

During the years I used the .375 H&H, one particular goal kept surfacing in my mind — a homemade bullet that would be as reliable on deer as any jacketed bullet. My first attempt at this, of course, was when I purchased the Lyman mould for the 375449 bullet.

Despite the fact that this is an excellent bullet, it is nothing more nor less than a .38-55 design adapted for the .375 H&H. As such it has a lot wrong with it. It doesn't feed too well through a bolt action, and one or two of the forward grease grooves are exposed when the bullet is seated, so that the gas check doesn't intrude into the powder chamber.

The 375449 bullet is, however, an accurate bullet, and if one can tolerate the two deficiencies just mentioned, it will do well in the deer woods. I never shot a deer with a cast bullet from the .375 H&H, but I did shoot a number of chucks with the Lyman bullet and once used it to clean out a family of wild dogs. I wasn't too enthused about shooting a family of dogs, but when told that it would either be my shooting or lethal poisoning, I figured the shooting would be far more merciful.

The dogs were holed up under some outbuildings on an old farm, so I went into the hayloft of the barn where

I could look down into the area where the dogs usually were. Sure enough, there were five of the half-grown pups. My bullets were fairly soft, pushed by 44.0 grains of IMR-3031 and a Cream of Wheat filler. I doubt that there was any expansion, but none was necessary. The bullet did its work quickly and efficiently without so much as a single yip.

After coming out of the barn, I spied the bitch loping for the woods. She was probably 60 to 75 yards out when the cast bullet struck her in the right hip, nearly taking the leg off and opening up the abdomen so that the intestines spilled out. She turned, snapping once at the wound before pitching over on the ground, dead before I reached her.

Although I never tried making copper driving bands from ⅜-inch copper tubing, I did obtain two or three sample ⅜-inch bronze washers which I placed in the mould before casting a bullet. I believe this idea would have worked had the washers had a larger hole through them and had they been .376-inch in diameter instead of .375, thus fitting the mould a bit better. With the smaller diameter, it was difficult to cast a bullet where the washer wasn't off to one side. Since the expense of having special washers made would have been prohibitive, I dumped the project and headed in a different direction. If I were at it today, I would certainly try the new Wilkes gas check as a driving band. I believe these gas checks would work better than the washers because they would heat up faster, allowing the bullet metal to fill out better in the mould. Further, the Wilkes gas check has a larger hole than the washers.

Sometime back around 1954 when I was still a bit smitten with the velocity bug, I acquired several pounds of Zamak (a zinc alloy) and proceeded to cast some bullets from it in my 375449 mould.

Now if you ever get the idea that you want to cast bullets of a zinc alloy — and there is lots to be said in favor of the idea — get a new melting pot, a new ladle and use a mould having very few grease grooves. Once you put zinc or a zinc alloy into a melting pot, that pot is forever contaminated with zinc, and even putting it into a coal furnace for hours on end will not cleanse it. I know, because I've been there. Yes, I'm still using the lead pot with a lead alloy, but there is no way I can turn the pot upside down and jar the frozen chunk of bullet metal loose should I want to use a different alloy. Once zinc has been used in a pot, any subsequent lead alloy will freeze fast to it.

Casting zinc alloy bullets from my 375449 mould was a real pain. The sprue had to be cut at the exact instant it froze or the metal would be so hard I had to beat the sprue plate to death with a club to cut the sprue. Even after the sprue was cut, the mould had to be beaten to jar the bullet loose from the blocks. If all this wasn't bad enough, there were times when I was melting the Zamak that it turned to slush and refused to pour. Perhaps it was overheated, but casting zinc alloy bullets from Zamak was a real hassle.

I did manage to cast quite a few zinc alloy bullets, and at that time there were some available commercially from the Western Alloy Company. The ones I cast were sized and lubricated in a Lyman 45 lubricator. I have long forgotten the size of the die used, but if I were to do it today, I would use an oversize die and merely lubricate the bullets. Trying to resize a zinc alloy bullet is nearly impossible.

There is a lot of room for experimentation with zinc alloy bullets, especially in rifles and calibers designed to give deep penetration. A zinc alloy bullet weighs about 60 percent of its lead counterpart and can be driven at top velocity. It will give deep penetration with little, if any, distortion, and will ricochet at the slightest excuse. In my limited testing, I loaded them with 72.0 grains of IMR-4320, but have no record of accuracy results nor of shooting chucks with them. One thing I do recall is that they did not foul the barrel.

About the same time I was working with the zinc alloy bullets, I also was working with an idea to swage bullet jackets from $\frac{3}{8}$-inch copper tubing. The jackets were to have a hole in the base so that they could be inserted into a smooth-sided mould and the metal poured through the base.

Al Horton made the dies for me. The jacket-forming die fitted into the top of my Hollywood press and consisted of a body having a ⅜-inch bore and a threaded stem that matched the inside diameter of the tubing. It was shorter than the die body by the thickness of the tubing.

In order to close the base of the jacket, Al made up a series of base dies to fit in the ram of the press. Each of these base dies had a tapered cavity, each at a different angle to close in the wall of the tubing. The final base die was perfectly flat.

In theory I should have been able to insert a length of annealed copper tubing onto the stem of the jacket forming die, the length of the tubing to extend far enough below the end of the stem to provide a base. Then I could bring each base die up against the tubing, gradually closing it in to form a base with a hole in it just large enough to match the sprue hole on the mould.

For some reason, it never worked properly. I could close the base of the jacket with the base dies, but never enough to leave just a small hole in the center. I was afraid that a large hole in the base would permit blowing the core from the jacket, leaving the jacket stuck in the barrel's bore. This then, was another project that never reached fruition although today you can purchase similar jackets and mould from NEI/Tooldyne of Portland, Oregon.

In 1958 my dissatisfaction with the design of the Lyman 375449 bullet and the desire to prove an idea prompted me to design three bullets for the .375 H&H. The bullets were to have a single, very shallow grease groove .0045-inch deep which would be covered when the bullet was seated with the gas check flush with the base of the neck. The moulds were cut by Lyman and numbered 375110, 375117 and 375118. These bullets are illustrated in *Handloader* No. 6.

The 375110 bullet was the heaviest of the lot, running about 300 grains in a 50/50 mixture of lead and wheelweights. This bullet was two-diameter, parallel-sided with a 90-degree point, making it a rifle-type wadcutter.

The 375118 bullet was the same length and had the same shank dimensions as the heavier bullet, but was pointed with a .500-inch radius ogive. It weighed 285 grains in the same 50/50 mixture.

The 375117 was a sharp spitzer bullet with a 1.250-inch radius ogive weighing about 250 grains. It was a poor design and not worth the bother of casting.

Although the 375110 and 375118 bullets both showed a lot of promise, the former would not feed through the bolt action due to its 90-degree point, and neither of them held enough lube in the shallow groove to stand the journey down the barrel. However, I want to point out that this was in the days before Alox. Since then I have used the 375110 bullet in the Ruger No. 3 Winchester .375 with 31.0 grains of IMR-3031 and obtained good accuracy.

In general the grease groove on all three bullets was too shallow, but the concept was sound and has been considerably improved upon by Dave Scovill and Svein Solli, the latter a hunter and shooter from Norway. Using bullet No. 375118 as a basis, Svein designed a new bullet for the .375 H&H now cataloged by NEI/Tooldyne as No. 280.375GC. Svein had the grease groove made a bit deeper and had the nose of the bullet shaped more like its roundnose jacketed counterpart. According to Svein, it feeds freely through the magazine. The grease groove is covered and stays inside of two inches at 100 yards when backed by 48.0 grains of IMR-3031. If I were looking for a conventional cast grooved bullet for the .375 H&H today, the NEI 280.375GC is the one I would choose.

Sometime during 1954 I figured that as long as I was going to carry an elephant rifle, I should have some bullets suitable for shooting elephants. There may have been some full jackets available at that time, but if so I wasn't aware of them, nor would I have spent the money if I had known of them. Instead, I sketched up a jacket design which, except for the lack of a grease groove and a gas check shank, was identical in size and shape to my later-designed 375110 cast bullet. Then I had a friend at the shop where I worked set up a screw machine and turn out about 100 jackets from brass bar stock. The jackets were $\frac{1}{16}$-inch thick.

After setting the jackets nose-down in a steel block having a series of holes drilled in it especially for that purpose, I filled each jacket with 40-60 solder, melting it with a propane torch. Loaded in front of 70.0 grains of IMR-4350, these bullets would penetrate 13½ inches of green oak across the grain. Seventy-six grains of the same powder would push the bullet through 18 inches of green oak, across the grain. I sent some of these bullets to Harry Zimmer who was in Africa at the time, but never heard that he used any of them.

About the same time I was making the full-jacketed bullets, I also stumbled onto an idea for making some cavity-point bullets, although why I wanted them, for the life of me I'll never know. At any rate, I took a handful of Speer 285-grain bullets and stood them base-down in the same steel block where I made the full jackets. With a propane torch, I heated the nose of each bullet until the core melted, then plunged the hollowpoint pin from my Lyman Gould mould into the nose of the Speer bullet until it stopped. By so doing, a certain amount of the molten core was displaced, leaving a deep cavity in the nose.

This was when I discovered that despite the fact that all the bullets in a box might look alike on the outside, they can be vastly different on the inside. Many of those old Speer bullets had burrs around the lip of the jacket which partially closed the nose opening and prevented the hollowpoint pin from entering. As soon as I saw this, I knew why there had been complaints about .30-caliber Speer bullets opening up on deer.

Fortunately, bullet manufacturers have initiated a considerable number of improvements over the years.and provide a much better product today than in the early 1950s. I use a lot of Speer bullets today and find them superb in every respect.

Still it would behoove the handloader, regardless of what bullet he is using, to saw a few bullets lengthwise and file them flat just to see what the jacket structure is on the inside and to note the hardness of the jacket. As I said earlier, different manufacturers produce bullets for different applications, and whereas one bullet might work fine for elk, it could fail miserably on deer, or vice versa.

I never shot anything with my cavity-point Speer bullets and gave up on the project when I discovered the cavities and subsequent bullet weights were not uniform.

In 1953 while I was still working with the Enfield, I discussed the practicality of paper patched bullets in the .375 H&H with Bert Armstrong. Bert's experience with rifles reached back into the 1880s and, although he was more of a shotgunner than a rifleman, he knew of things of which I had never heard. Not only did Bert believe the idea to be feasible, but he produced an old Ideal handbook that showed a cutaway drawing of the Ideal Cylindrical Adjustable mould for paper patched bullets. This same drawing also was reproduced in the *Ideal Handbook No. 39*, page 182.

I'm not all that great as a machinist, and the machine I operated nights at the plant where I worked wasn't in the best condition. Yet by dint of perseverance I managed to whittle a bullet mould from a piece of mild steel, though the reamer chattered so badly that the resulting bullet had about 16 sides on it. The bullet weighed 330 grains and when patched with .002-inch thick paper, measured .374-inch in diameter.

Backed by 49.0 grains of surplus IMR-4895, and the air space filled with cornmeal, I fired a few two-inch groups with this bullet as well as some six- or eight-inch groups.

Had I pursued the matter a bit further, I might have reached my goal of producing a good homemade hunting bullet about 30 years earlier than I did. It wasn't until the 1980s that I really got into paper patched bullets again and found out what makes them work and what makes them fail.

Although I much prefer a smooth-sided, cupped-base paper patched bullet, any good conventional grooved cast bullet can be paper patched and made into a better hunting bullet than when without the patch.

When most people think of a paper patched bullet, they equate it with black powder and buffalo, and certainly it earned an enviable reputation in that setting. Basically, however, a paper patched bullet is a paper jacketed bullet and enjoys all the advantages, plus a few more, of a metal-jacketed bullet up to about 2,200 fps or a bit over. The one drawback is that it is more time consuming to patch a bullet than it is to run it through a sizer-lubricator, and people today simply find it easier to follow the path of least resistance.

My Ruger No. 1 .375 H&H with its freebore was made to order for using paper patched bullets, but still lacking a good paper patched bullet mould for that caliber, I resorted to the next best thing and patched some of my regular cast bullets with a nine-pound onionskin. Naturally, this increased the bullet's diameter, but as long as I could chamber them, they showed considerable promise. Such oversized patched bullets did have a bad fault of leaving a hard ring of paper in front of the chamber, thus interfering with the next round.

This problem was easily overcome by lubricating the patched bullet with a mixture of 45 percent beeswax and 55 percent clear Vaseline™, and then running it through a .376-inch die in my SAECO sizer-lubricator. This operation irons the patch to a hard surface and also presses some of the lube into the patch. Most important, it reduces the outside diameter of the patched bullet so that it is compatible with the chamber and no longer leaves a ring of paper in the barrel.

Using this system of patching on my shallow-groove bullets 375110 and 375118 and the Lyman 375449, I was able to come up with superb hunting loads. With the 375110 I used 47.0 grains of IMR-3031 with a Cream of Wheat filler for an average of 1,982 fps. The bullet weighed 302 grains and was very accurate.

For those who are impressed by energy figures, that amounts to 2,627 foot-pounds of energy — in the same bracket as the .30-06 — and with a bullet far softer than the conventional cast bullet.

Later Charlie Canoll made an adjustable paper patched bullet mould for me, and I made up some soft bullets — pure lead with 3 percent tin — weighing 310 grains. Backed by 47.0 grains of IMR-3031 with a Cream of Wheat filler, these bullets averaged 1,982 fps with an extreme spread of only 18 fps. For deer hunting, they would be superb.

Following the 1975 season, I never carried the .375 H&H deer hunting again. The rifle was simply getting too heavy to carry. So beginning with the 1976 season I went to the Ruger No. 1 .45-70 and have carried it or my No. 3 ever since. I must confess that I miss my .375 H&H and consider it the best of any cartridge I ever used on deer.

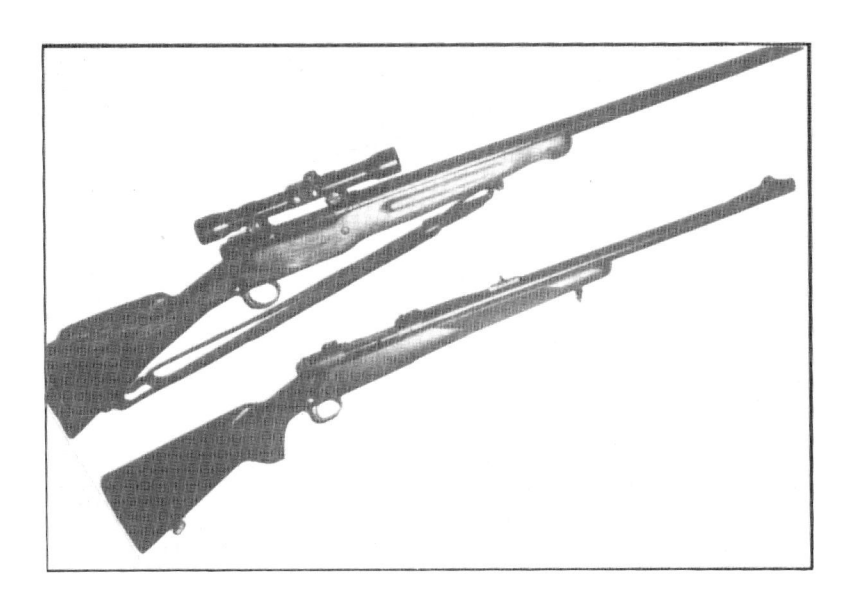

A pair of .375 H&H magnums. The Enfield that Charlie built for me is at the top, while my Winchester with iron sights and Weaver top detachable mounts is at the bottom.

Spike buck taken in 1953 with the Winchester .375 H&H and a 255-grain Remington .38-55 bullet.

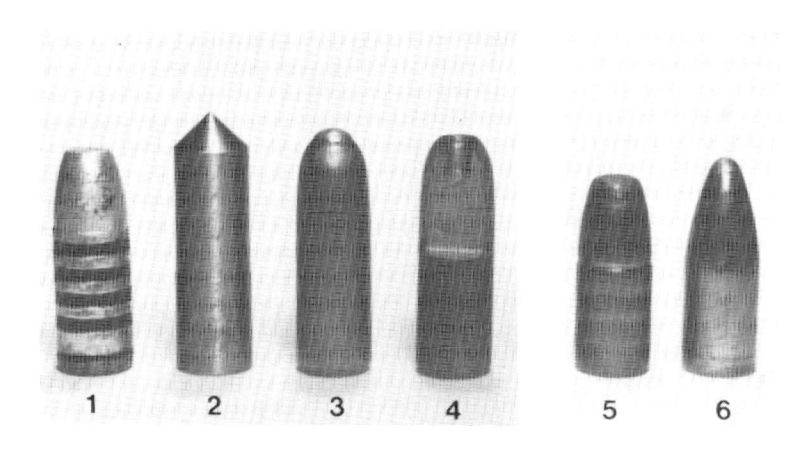

Bullets for the .375 H&H Magnum. Left to right: (1) zinc alloy bullet cast in the Lyman 375449 mould, (2) brass-jacketed FMJ bullet made by the author, (3) Barnes 300-grain softnose, (4) sectioned Barnes bullet with 1/8-inch diameter hollowpoint, (5) Winchester 255 FMJ .38-55 bullet, and (6) the Speer 235-grain bullet.

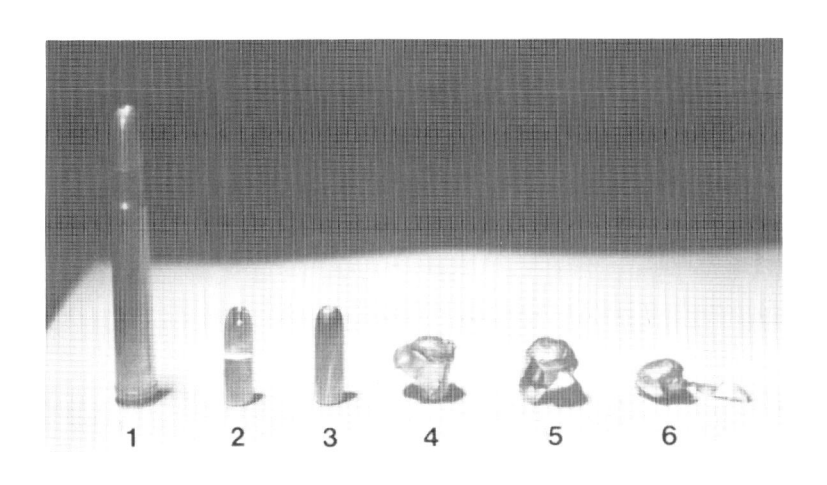

Left to right: (1) .375 H&H cartridge loaded with Barnes 300-grain bullet hollowpointed with 1/8-inch center drill; (2) sectioned hollowpoint bullet; (3) same bullet after being fired into gelatin block with 80 grains of DuPont Fg black powder; (4) same bullet fired with 40 grains of 4895 (lot 27,277) (249 grains recovered); (5) bullet fired with 50 grains of IMR-4895 (198 grains recovered); (6) bullet fired with 70 grains of IMR-4350 (154 grains recovered). The maximum penetration in sawdust after passing through the gelatin was 40 inches with the black powder load. Minimum penetration in the sawdust was 13½ inches with 70 grains of IMR-4350.

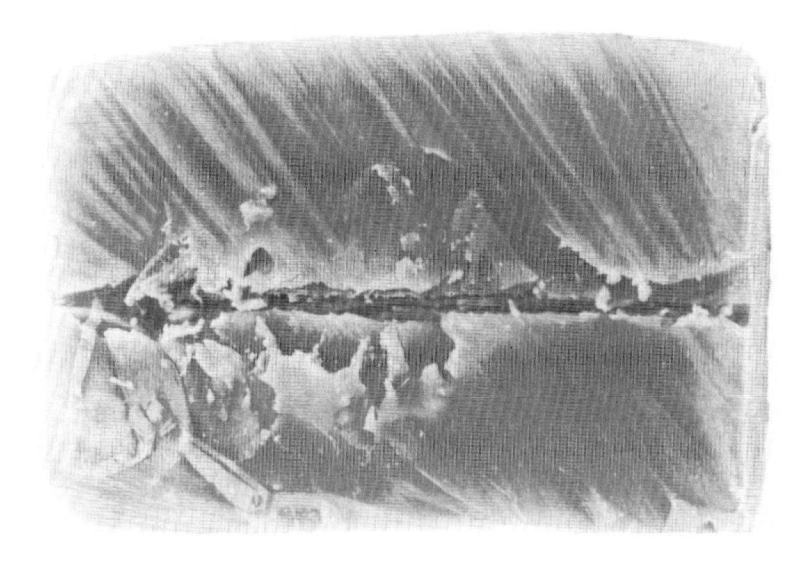

Wound channel through nine-inch gelatin block with hollow-pointed Barnes bullet backed with 76.0 grains of IMR-4350. Range was 75 yards. The snow behind the gelatin was specked with tiny particles of lead and jacket.

Six .375 H&H cartridges loaded with cast bullets. Left to right: (1) Lyman 375110 seated out for single shot; (2) Lyman 375110 seated to cover the grease groove; (3) Lyman 375118; (4) Lyman 375117; (5) Lyman 375449; and (6) Lyman 37583, a fine bullet for small game when loaded with a light charge of Bullseye.

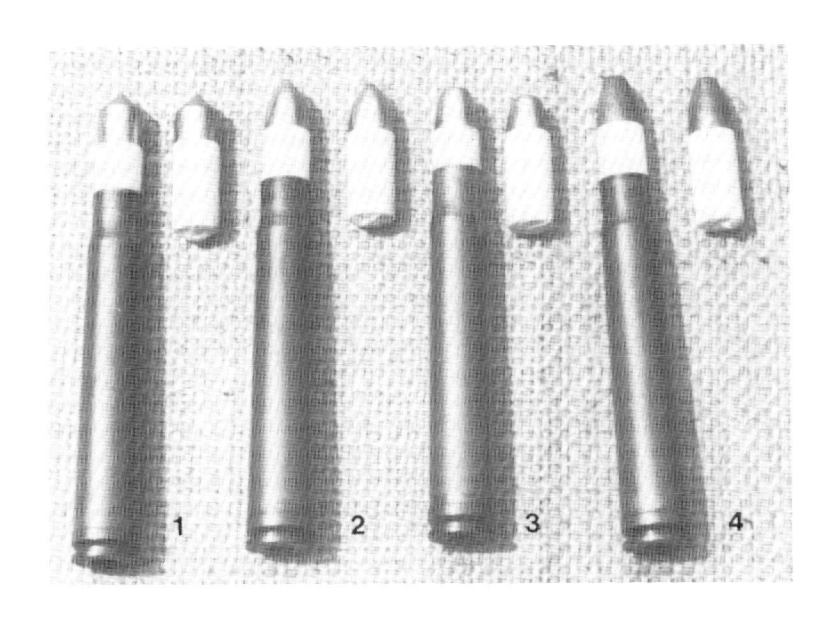

Four .375 H&H cartridges loaded with paper patched bullets. Left to right: (1) Lyman 375110, (2) 375118, (3) 375449, and (4) a bullet from a mould cut by Charlie Canoll. All bullets are patched with a nine-pound onionskin paper. The Lyman bullets were run through a .376-inch SAECO sizing die *after* being patched and lubricated.

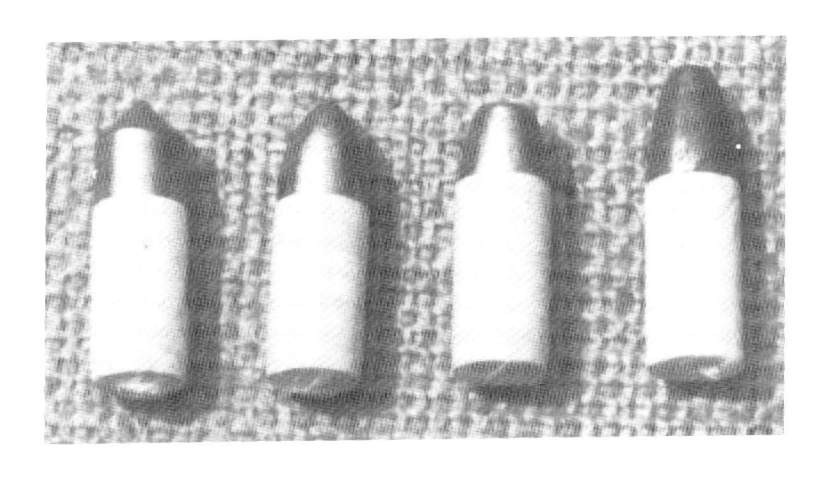

The same .375 paper patched bullets as shown in previous photo.

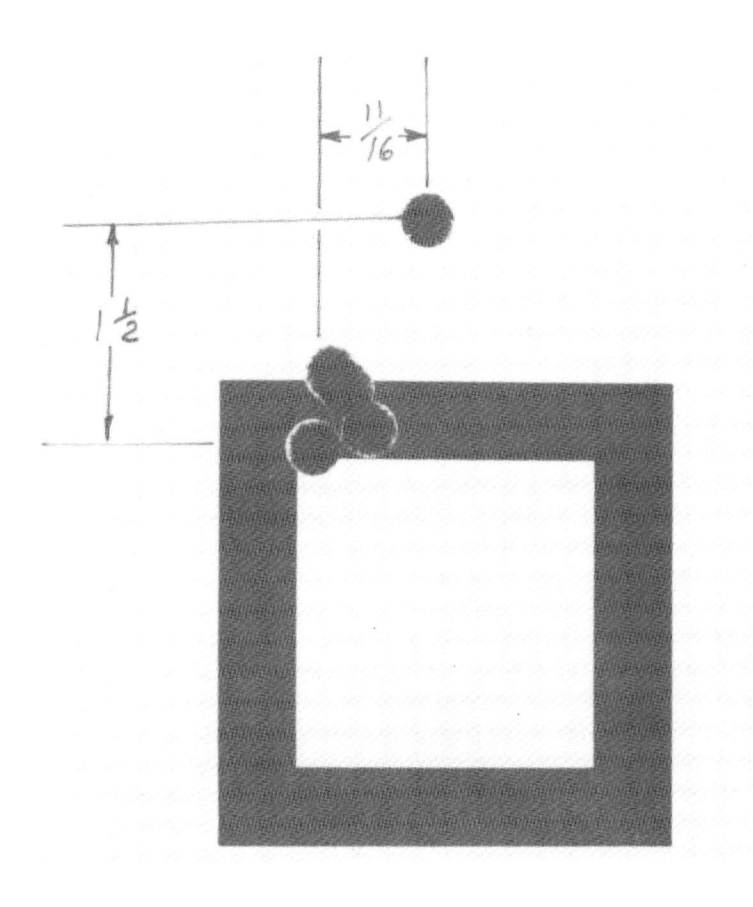

Target fired with the Lyman 375110 paper patched bullet. Good enough for any deer in the country!

9

The .45-70s

The .45-70 is the greatest woods cartridge ever developed. Because of the wide variety of cast bullet designs available — everything from a roundball to a 550-grain paper patched bullet — the old government workhorse has a versatility second to none and a capability far beyond that recognized by most gunscribes.

If we look back at the heyday of elephant hunting, we find that John "Pondoro" Taylor shot his first tusker with a Martini .577-450 throwing a 480-grain .45-caliber bullet backed by 85.0 grains of black powder for a velocity of 1,350 fps, not too different from the original .45-70-500, and easily surpassed with a smokeless load in a Ruger No. 1. Then there was Frederick Courteney Selous who considered the .450 Black Powder Express to be a superb elephant rifle. According to Taylor, one of the favorite loads in the .450 BPE was a 365-grain bullet backed by 120 grains of black powder for a velocity of 1,700 fps. In Selous' book *Travel and Adventure in South-East Africa* he writes of using the .450 BPE with a 540-grain hardened bullet backed by 75.0 grains of black powder. Velocity couldn't have been anything over 1,250 fps, and maybe not that much.

By contrast the Ruger No. 1 can throw a 540-grain paper patched bullet at least 1,600 fps. So although it is not by any means a .458 Winchester Magnum, a man wouldn't have to feel undergunned with a good .45-70 provided he had the means of loading his own cartridges.

At the other end of the scale, one of the best tin-can, rock-busting, easy-shooting loads I ever used in a .45-70 was 10.0 grains of Unique behind a 300- to 355-grain bullet with the air space *filled* with a tuft of Dacron a half-inch square and about 1½ inches long. (When I first started using Dacron, I purchased it in the form of pillow stuffing. Then I learned to purchase the ½-inch batting and found it much easier to cut each filling to a specific size.)

This load gives about 940 fps and is very accurate out to about 75 yards. Although it may seem anemic, it is more powerful than any load one would care to use in a .45 Colt, certainly adequate for deer if a man is capable of doing his hunting in the 10- to 30-yard range.

To go even farther down the scale, I've fired many rounds using 3.8 grains of Bullseye behind almost any bullet from 300 up to 420 grains. This load sounds about like a .22 Short and is plenty accurate out to 25 yards. Beyond that, forget it, but for a job that has to be done without arousing the neighbors, this little whisper load will punch a man-size hole at a velocity of about 450 fps and with little fuss.

I acquired my first .45-70 rifle in May 1950, a Winchester Model 1886 that had been rebarreled and chambered by Parker O. Ackley. It didn't take too long after that to learn that the .45-70 was a whale of a cartridge. It would drive a 405-grain jacketed bullet into the vitals of a deer from any angle, something I had learned was impossible with lightweight, fast-stepping projectiles from the .30-06.

I also learned that the .45-70 is not a cross-field cartridge as was the '06, nor is it a desirable cartridge for shooting at running game. While most gunscribes point a critical finger at the rainbow trajectory of the .45-70, trajectory is no problem for the type of hunting in which a .45-70 would normally be used — that is, woods hunting where a 125-yard shot is a long shot. Here a good .45-70 loaded with a 400-grain bullet pushed by 53.0 grains of IMR-3031 can be sighted to strike two inches high at 100 yards and be on the money at 125 yards.

The real problem with the .45-70 in the game field is the amount of lead required to make a good hit on running game. The time of flight at 50 yards for a .45-70 bullet leaving the muzzle at 1,800 fps is about .086 second, with the heavier bullets taking milliseconds less time than the lighter bullets. During that time of flight, a deer running 25 mph covers almost three feet, and a man sighting on the chest area could miss the animal entirely, or worse, inflict a nasty wound too far back.

For those who do a lot of shotgunning on running game, lead is a lot less of a problem. Years ago I knew a man who was a superb shotgunner and what I would call an expert on the running game shot. It made little difference to him whether he was using a single-barreled shotgun with rifled slugs, or a lever-action 99 Savage; give him a shot at a running deer within the normal woods ranges, and he would pile the deer up on the first shot.

I recall the first time I showed Penny my Winchester 1886. He threw it to his shoulder a few times and finally remarked that he believed he could shoot that rifle. I handed him one of my heavy loads, threw a bottle into the air and stood there open-mouthed as he pulverized it.

I was never that good, not with a shotgun and not with a rifle on running game. Since I quit using the shotgun for small game over 15 years ago, what little ability I had acquired is gone. For me to lead a running deer with a rifle requires a conscious effort, a determination of exactly where to put the crosshairs in relation to the front of the deer. Penny did it by instinct borne of many years of shooting with a shotgun.

I shot deer with the Winchester using both the Gould hollowpoint and a 405-grain jacketed bullet. Betty shot deer with the rifle and so did my son, and it didn't take too long to recognize its capabilities in the deer woods.

Thus it was that when the weight of my .375 H&H began to become too much, I purchased a Ruger No. 3 .45-70 in 1975 and a Ruger No. 1 chambered for the same cartridge in 1976. Although the Ruger No. 1 was a bit heavier than the No. 3, it was significantly lighter than my No. 1 .375 H&H and handled much better. In fact, I believe that for easy handling and natural pointability, the Ruger No. 1 .45-70 with its 22-inch medium-weight barrel and short forend is probably the best I've ever used. With a high quality 2½x fixed power scope like the Leupold Compact mounted on the rib, it can hardly be surpassed as a woods rifle.

The .45-70 cartridge is a natural for cast bullets. After all, it was designed for a lead alloy bullet in an era when all bullets were either cast or swaged of a lead alloy. If there is any problem with cast bullets, it is in the fact that some of our mould manufacturers base the weight of the bullet on Linotype and cut their moulds accordingly. Thus, a mould listed as casting a 400-grain bullet is quite likely to cast a bullet weighing 420 to 425 grains when using an alloy soft enough to expand.

Although there is considerable justification in cutting moulds for the smallbores based on Linotype, there is no justification whatsoever for using a Linotype bullet in the .45-70 when a much softer and more economical bullet will serve as well on the target and better on game. Furthermore, when you start adding unnecessary weight to large bullets — even at modest velocities — recoil is increased significantly and unnecessarily. More than that, if that extra weight is added to the base of the bullet instead of the nose, case capacity sometimes is reduced to the point that efficiency of the cartridge is badly impaired.

A case in point is the RCBS 45-500-FN bullet. All of the weight in this bullet is on its back end so that when seated to the crimping groove, it will feed through the Marlin 1895SS action. By the time the bullet is seated that deeply in the case, however, there is not enough case capacity left to make it worthwhile in any .45-70. Had the shank of that bullet been left the same length as the 45-400-FN bullet and the extra weight added to the nose, then the bullet could have been used to good advantage in one of the single shots.

I want to point out that the .45-caliber RCBS bullets are very accurate and that I have used a number of those from the 45-500-FN mould in my Ruger No. 1 .458 Magnum.

The RCBS 45-300-FN bullet is one of the finest lightweight cast bullets available for the .45-70. It is excellent as a light-load bullet with 10.0 grains of Unique and a Dacron filler, although a gas checked bullet isn't necessary for that application. The little RCBS bullet weighs about 319 grains when cast of a soft alloy and about 312 grains when cast of 75 percent wheelweights and 25 percent pure lead. Loaded in front of 32.0 grains of 2400 it gives an average velocity of 1,711 fps and is devastating on deer if placed up front where it can smash bones. I'm not certain if the mixture of wheelweights and lead is soft enough to guarantee expansion, and I long ago gave up the idea that a .45-caliber bullet is already large enough without expansion. If you want *consistently* reliable performance on deer, the bullet must readily expand without shedding a lot of weight.

The RCBS 45-300-FN bullet delivers good accuracy and helps promote low recoil, but again, when dealing with cast bullets, one can usually drive a heavy bullet at the same or greater velocity than a light bullet and usually with better accuracy. With bullets of the same overall design — as with the RCBS .45-caliber rifle bullets — this is because of a longer bearing surface with adequate lubricant.

The RCBS 45-400-FN is a superb all-around-use cast bullet, especially for the Marlin 1895SS. Like the other two RCBS bullets, it has enough bearing surface in front of the leading driving band to fill the freebore ahead of the Ruger chamber bringing it close to the origin of the rifling. When seated to the crimping groove, the overall cartridge length is just right for the Marlin. If I was buying a mould specifically for use in the Marlin, the RCBS

45-400-FN would be the one, even though it casts a heavy 425 grains when a soft alloy is used.

Loading for the Ruger single shot .45-70 offers all kinds of opportunities for practically any .45-caliber rifle bullet in existence. By not having to accommodate a magazine, overall cartridge length is governed only by the bullet design and throat dimensions, allowing one to use such old designs as the Lyman 457132 Postell bullet. This is a long-nose bullet designed as a grooved counterpart of the Sharps 550-grain paper patched bullet. The nose diameter just ahead of the front driving band measures about .444 inch making it suitable for use with black powder loads when you're not cleaning between shots, or with Pyrodex where cleaning between shots is unnecessary.

Until I had used black powder in my single shots, I didn't realize the significance of the difference in nose diameters of bullets from various manufacturers. I often had wondered why some of the old Lyman bullets — and some of their newer bullets based on old designs — had small nose diameters, while most of the more recent manufacturers went along with the more modern concept of a .450-inch nose diameter.

The reason becomes quickly apparent when you try to chamber one of the larger diameters in a barrel that has been fouled with black powder. The fouling in the throat and origin of the rifling usually interferes with bullets having the full .450-inch diameter nose unless the bore is cleaned after each shot.

This difference in nose diameters is of considerable importance when ordering a custom mould. If the bullet is to be used strictly with smokeless powder, a nose diameter that closely matches the rifle's bore diameter helps promote better accuracy. If the bullet is to be used with black powder — and a lot of shooters are going in that direction today — then much thought should be given toward the smaller nose diameter or a Pope-style bullet with a short nose.

This same difference carries over into paper patched bullets. For my Rugers and smokeless powder, I like a paper patched bullet having an *unpatched* diameter of .452 inch. This is just about .0005 inch larger than the bore diameter of the rifles and lets me use a paper patched bullet of any hardness I want from pure lead to Linotype. Once the barrel is fouled with black powder, however, there is no way I can chamber a cartridge loaded with a paper patched bullet having an unpatched diameter of .452 inch and a patched diameter of about .459 inch. For black powder use, the *unpatched* diameter of the bullet should be approximately .446 to .448 inch.

In addition to the Lyman and RCBS moulds mentioned, I acquired a number of other moulds for use with the Ruger single-shot rifles. One of my favorites was the NEI/Tooldyne 430.458GC, or NEI Smasher as I like to call it. This bullet is shaped a lot like the Lyman 457483 bullet, but is slightly heavier, has wider driving bands and the larger .450-inch diameter nose. If I was going after the big stuff with a Ruger .45-70 and the conventional cast bullet, this is the one I would probably use.

Old West offers a superb bullet cataloged as No. .460350GC. This was designed especially for the new Marlin 1895 and the Winchester or Browning 1886 lever actions. It has a truncated cone nose that lets it feed through the action like corn through a goose, and a generous meplat that allows it to be used in a tubular magazine with little chance of chain firing. I've used this bullet a lot in the Rugers and found it superbly accurate and a bit easier in the recoil department than the heavier bullets. Thirty-three grains of 2400 pushes this bullet along at 1,746 fps from my Ruger No. 3 with its 22-inch barrel.

I later had Richard Hoch cut two moulds for me, one plain base and the other with a gas-check shank. Both bullets were patterned after the Old West design, but were about 10 grains heavier — 355 grains — and had wider grease grooves. When loaded in front of 44.0 grains of IMR-4198, the gas-checked bullet gave slightly better than

1,800 fps with superb accuracy. I use the plain base bullet a lot with my practice load of 10.0 grains of Unique and Dacron filler.

There is one thing about cast bullets that should be mentioned right here — the perfect base. When you shoot a cast bullet that has a lump on the base due to a poor and/or dull sprue cutter, or a cavity in the base where overly hot metal was pulled out, you are wasting time, powder, primer and bullet metal. The base of a cast bullet must be absolutely perfect for good results. There is no more perfect base than that provided by a nose-pour mould.

This is not to say that you can't get a good base from a base-pour mould, because you can. I do it all the time. I cast slow and give the sprue plenty of time to harden so that I don't pull a chunk of metal from the bullet's base. I try to get moulds that have a thick, heavy sprue cutter.

As far as I'm concerned, casting good rifle bullets is not a race against time to see how many I can cast. As mentioned I learned that after my first casting session with the Ideal 3118 bullet when Charlie Canoll picked 15 or 20 good bullets out of the 400 that I had cast. Today I take my time and produce about 75 bullets per hour. After they are all done, even bullets up in the 425-grain weight range won't vary much more than +.5 grain.

For hunting purposes, I believe there is no better home-grown cast bullet available than the paper patched variety. I believe this is true simply because the paper patched bullet can be made as soft as desired, even of pure lead, and still be driven at velocities of 1,800 to 2,200 fps with good accuracy. There is no way that can be duplicated or even approached with the conventional cast bullet which by necessity requires that its entire shank be hard enough to withstand barrel friction to prevent leading.

With the exception of only a few designs, the paper patched bullet itself never touches the barrel — only the patch which prevents leading. In fact, the paper patched bullet leaves no metal fouling whatsoever in the barrel, and you needn't worry about the lubricant freezing in the winter or melting in the summer. It is an ideal hunting bullet that can be made soft enough to expand all the way from about 800 fps to the muzzle velocity of the rifle, and due to the lead's molecular cohesion it won't break up unless you add antimony to it.

I have fired thousands of paper patched bullets from my .45-70s. I've shot deer and wild hogs with them, and if I'm lucky, I'll take a black bear in Canada with a soft paper patched bullet backed by 53.0 grains of IMR-3031.

Charlie Canoll made my first bullet mould for a .45-caliber paper patched bullet. It was adjustable for bullet length, had a cupped base to accommodate the tail end of the patch, and cast a bullet with an unpatched diameter of .450-inch. I then asked Dave Farmer of Colorado Shooter's Supply to make me a similar mould which would cast a bullet measuring .452-inch across the waist.

Both moulds are superb, although when I'm casting with any metal harder than pure lead for use with smokeless powder, it is important that I use the larger diameter bullet or else the patch will be stripped from the bullet while in the barrel and the barrel will be badly leaded. Smokeless powder just doesn't bump the bullet enough to take the rifling.

Since I wrote the book *The Practical Paper Patched Bullet*, I have learned one or two additional items which are significant in using paper patched bullets. First, I cut all of my patches *across* the paper grain. Because the paper will stretch more when cut in this direction, the patch must be 1/32 to 1/16-inch shorter than one cut with the grain. Most important, however, the patch cut across the grain will shrink to a uniform fit all around the bullet where it extends a bit beyond the ogive's origin, whereas the patch cut with the grain will not shrink as much and will pucker in two or three places where it overlaps the ogive's origin.

The second thing I've learned is to use a patch that overhangs the base just far enough to be twisted and which will totally cover the surface of the cupped base. That is, don't make the patch long enough to create a tail — just long enough to twist and cover the base cavity. Doing it this way eliminates any indentation into the base caused by the powder slamming into the hard knot of paper formed by the twisted tail.

I have also taken a cue from Harry Pope and am now using a thin card wad between the powder and the bullet's base. This is particularly important with very soft bullets, because the powder slamming into the base at the instant of ignition makes tiny imprints all over the base of the bullet including the rim of the cavity. This doesn't help accuracy. Harry Pope used to save old postcards for such wads, but posterboard obtained at a stationery store will work just as well. The important thing is to use a hard-surfaced wad that is as light as possible. I've always believed that heavy wads behind a bullet do nothing to enhance accuracy.

When I wrote the book *Forty Years with the .45-70*, I had just obtained a new Marlin 1895SS with the idea of learning whether or not the Micro-Groove rifling would handle paper patched bullets. This was one of the newer models with the cross-bolt safety, and surprisingly enough, when I slugged the barrel, I found that it was a shade tighter than my Rugers on both the bore diameter and the groove diameter. This meant that the grooves were as deep on the Marlin, if not a shade deeper, than on my single shots. Now whether or not Marlin has made a change in their barrel specifications, I don't know, but I do know that my Marlin and a number of others being used in Alaska handle cast bullets exceedingly well.

This should be a great boost to the Marlin rifle, because for years cast bullet shooters, myself included, shied away from the 1895 because of its Micro-Groove rifling. Although it probably won't win any benchrest awards at the cast bullet matches, the Marlin 1895SS will throw fairly soft cast bullets (6 to 7 BHN) into three inches or less — usually much less — at 100 yards with no problem. For the type of hunting and shooting for which the rifle is designed, this is more than adequate.

My nephew, Fred von Wolffradt, who is stationed in Alaska and uses a Marlin 1895SS .45-70, has told me that many Alaskans purchased the Marlin as a second rifle — a knockabout working gun. After using it a few times, however, they discovered that they didn't need any other rifle. When I asked Fred what their "first" rifles were, he told me, ".375s and .458s!"

Returning to my tests with the Marlin, I found that it handled paper patched bullets as well as any other .45-70, although overall cartridge length coupled with bullet design sometimes predicated a slightly lower load than my usual 53.0 grains of IMR-3031. With a fairly short bullet weighing 367 grains I was able to use the 53.0 grain load, but with the longer 400-grain bullet having a blunt nose, I had to cut the charge to 50.0 grains. Even so, the average velocity was 1,781 fps with an extreme spread of only 19 fps.

In order to prevent damage to the patch while going through the loading gate, there are two or three different things that can be done. First, it helps to waterproof the patches by cooking the patched bullets in melted beeswax — no other type of wax — for 10 minutes, then rolling them back and forth on paper towels to remove the excess, and finally rubbing them down with finely powdered graphite. Let the bullets cool for a day or so before loading. This allows the beeswax to shrink so that it doesn't stick to the bullet.

Secondly, don't extend the patch any farther ahead of the mouth of the cartridge case than necessary. In fact, when I finished working with paper patched bullets in the Marlin, I was regulating the width of my patch so that when the bullet was seated, *all* of the patch was inside the cartridge case. This gave the patch full protection. When I did this I used a 423-grain bullet so that I had lots of bearing surface. The powder charge was 46½ grains of IMR-3031.

As for conventional cast grooved bullets in the Marlin, I like the RCBS 45-400-FN bullet cast of a soft alloy (6 to 7 BHN) pushed by 46½ grains of IMR-3031. This bullet weighs about 425 grains, has a lot of bearing surface and is plenty accurate. Its flat nose makes it a natural for the tubular magazine as well as transmitting energy to the game. When my nephew was home for deer season, we cast and lubricated 100 of these bullets to take back to Alaska. The lubricant was the standard 50/50 Alox/beeswax mix and was used at temperatures to 10 degrees below zero with no problems. Fred and some of his Alaskan friends are using a slightly heavier load, 48.0 grains of IMR-3031 with the RCBS bullet.

When I first got into heavy use of paper patched bullets, I used a Lyman M-die to open the mouth of the case prior to seating a bullet. The M-die worked fairly well as long as the patched diameter of the bullet was within the die's diameter, but if the patched diameter was a bit big and the paper thin, then the patch was sometimes torn.

For proper seating of a paper patched bullet, the case mouth should be opened with a gentle flare. For this purpose, I had Charlie Canoll modify my RCBS neck expanding plug to incorporate a short tapered section having a 1½-degree taper to open the case mouth. This worked so well for paper patched bullets, that I now use the flaring die instead of the M-die to facilitate seating regular cast bullets. I usually flare the case enough so that a bullet can be hand seated to cover the gas check and the bottom driving band. Sometimes I even seat the bullet to full depth by hand.

For cartridges to be used in the Marlin, after seating the bullet I remove the decapping pin assembly from the .45-70 full-length resizing die and run the loaded cartridge into the die just far enough to remove all evidence of the flare. This helps the cartridge to feed better from the magazine into the chamber.

I do not remove the flare from cartridges being used in the single shots unless the cartridges are for hunting purposes. However slight the flare is, I believe it helps center the mouth of the cartridge in the front of the chamber, thus promoting better accuracy. How much this helps, or if it really helps, I cannot say, but it certainly cannot do any harm.

About the same time that I was doing serious work with the Marlin, it dawned on me that I never had really worked with Pyrodex powder. Oh, I had fired a few rounds through a rolling block using the CTG Pyrodex, but not enough to amount to anything.

First, I must return to my earlier comment about using full-diameter bullets with straight black powder loads. In most cases when this is done, the black powder fouling in the throat or leade of the barrel interferes with chambering a cartridge unless the bullet is seated well back from the rifling's origin. Even then, a full bore-diameter nose on the bullet can give problems.

This condition can be alleviated by using a duplex load involving a priming charge of SR-4759 to help burn off the solids left by the black. My priming charges were about 12 or 13 percent by weight of the original black powder load. Thus, for the .45-70, based on a 70-grain charge, I used eight to 10 grains of SR-4759 as a priming charge.

Warning: When a priming charge is used, chamber pressures are significantly increased and could be dangerous in original or replica rifles designed for use with black powder. I do not recommend the use of a priming charge, but merely relate what I did in my Ruger rifles to reduce the black powder fouling.

In addition to the increase in chamber pressures, loading duplex loads is a nuisance. You always have to deal with two powders and run the risk of a double priming charge. The use of Pyrodex eliminates this. Although Pyrodex fouls the barrel more severely than a duplex load, the fouling is not cumulative, (i.e., it doesn't build up in the barrel as does black powder fouling). It will, however, still cause interference when chambering cartridges loaded with certain bullets unless the barrel is cleaned after every shot.

When I first started using Pyrodex, I used the CTG grade intended for cartridge rifles. My first container, the rectangular can, indicated that it was similar to FFg black powder. Subsequent containers were of the black plastic bottle type and indicated that the CTG Pyrodex is similar to Fg, while the RS Pyrodex is similar to FFg. This is the way I find the two powders in actual use. It also is my experience that the CTG Pyrodex will not "bump" an undersize bullet up to fill the rifling grooves, whereas the RS Pyrodex works nicely in this respect. It might also be worth mentioning here that I prefer using Magnum primers with Pyrodex.

Using Pyrodex in the .45-70 has significant advantages. First, ever since I got into handloading back in 1949, there has been a continuous, although rather subdued, request for the powder companies to introduce a true bulk smokeless powder for use in black powder cartridge rifles. Although the powder manufacturers claimed that such an animal was impossible to produce, along came Dan Pawlak, self-taught in the field of pyrotechnics, who developed a true bulk powder purposely made to create a degree of smoke and soot to satisfy the charcoal burners!

Although I would prefer a true bulk smokeless, Pyrodex is the next best thing. Due to its higher ignition temperature, it is safer to handle than black powder, and being a bulk-for-bulk equivalent of black, there is no way one can double-charge a cartridge case when using the proper grade of Pyrodex. For the man who wants an easy shooting load, which is perfectly reliable as a game killer, is accurate and which creates no concern about pressure limits and excessive charges, Pyrodex is the way to go. The more I use it, the better I like it.

As far as bullet lubricant is concerned, I wipe all my paper patched bullets with a 45/55 mixture of beeswax and Vaseline^{TM}. Just a thin film of this lube wiped on the patch and the bullet's nose leaves a moist ring around the rifle's muzzle. On my regular cast bullets, I use either the standard Alox/beeswax mixture or Rooster Laboratories'

HVR lube, whichever happens to be in the SAECO sizer-lubricator at the time. However, if I was to have a sizer-lubricator set up expressly for black powder or Pyrodex shooting, I would use the same beeswax/Vaseline™ mixture I use on my paper patched bullets. I use hand-lubed grooved bullets with this and it works fine.

As with any other powder, there always are certain loading techniques to be used. First, regardless of whether I'm using black powder, Pyrodex or smokeless, I weigh all of my charges, and any load mentioned herein is by weight to less than .1 grain.

Secondly, I don't put Pyrodex (or black) in a powder measure. I tried Pyrodex in my old Hollywood measure (circa 1950) and two days later I had to remove the drum and clean it to get it to function. Fired or unfired, Pyrodex is corrosive, at least to some metals. When charging cases with Pyrodex, I usually fill my powder dribbler and then use an old shotshell powder and shot dipper to dip a charge of powder directly from the bottle to the pan on the scales. A few kernels of powder are then dribbled onto the pan to bring it up to the proper weight.

Pyrodex weighs about 80 percent that of black powder. That is, 56 grains of Pyrodex take up the same volume as 70 grains of black, and since most .45-70 cases won't hold 70 grains of black, neither will they hold 56 grains of Pyrodex unless the powder is dribbled in slowly, slightly compressed and the bullet seated well out. If you just dump the powder into the case, 54 grains usually fills it to brimming.

There are three different ways of getting Pyrodex into the case and still have room left to seat a bullet. The first is to use a drop tube such as a 36-inch faucet supply, that lets the powder settle into the smallest possible space. Even then, it may have to be compressed somewhat to fully seat the bullet.

The second way is to funnel the powder into the case and then compress it with a wooden or steel dowel. The third method is to funnel the powder into the case and compress it as the bullet is seated. I know this is done, because I've had people tell me about it, but a loading press has a lot of leverage, and all that force can't help but distort the bullet and probably the bullet's base where it contacts the Pyrodex. It is not a method I would recommend.

For quite a while I compressed my Pyrodex-loaded cases with a steel dowel. Since I couldn't easily regulate the exact depth or amount of compression, however, I devised another way. First, I got a .35 Remington case with the spent primer still in place. The head of the .35 Remington will just fit inside the .45-70 case. Then, using a Lyman 310 decapping chamber with the decapping pin removed, I slipped the .35 Remington case up over the stem of the die and slid the charged .45-70 case into the shellholder underneath. A gentle push on the handle of the press compressed the Pyrodex to the exact depth I wanted, which was indicated by a line scribed or inked on the .35 Remington case. This method works absolutely perfect for me.

One of the handiest accessories I ever purchased was a reducing die purchased from Dave Corbin of White City, Oregon. I got it for the specific purpose of reducing the diameter of my regular cast bullets from .460 to .452 inch so that I could paper patch every .45-caliber bullet for which I had a mould. The system works well and the Corbin reducing die will easily reduce the diameter of a cast bullet by .008 inch and still maintain concentricity.

After I started using Pyrodex, I found another application for the reducing die. As I mentioned earlier, whether using black powder or Pyrodex there is a sufficient amount of fouling in the throat and barrel to interfere with bullets having a .450-inch diameter nose or a paper patched bullet having a patched diameter of .458 or .459 inch.

Keeping this in mind, I took some full-diameter paper patched bullets, lubricated them with my standard lube, and shoved them nose-first through the reducing die. They came out .453-inch. Loaded over 54.0 or 56.0 grains of

RS Pyrodex they chamber without a hitch and easily slug up in the bore to deliver good accuracy. By using the Corbin reducing die, I have doubled the practical use of every .45-caliber mould I own, and can adapt each bullet for either smokeless powder, Pyrodex or black.

One of the best conventional cast bullets I've used with Pyrodex is the RCBS 45-300-FN. This bullet actually weighs much heavier when cast of a soft alloy, and has a full caliber of bearing surface. Yet, when seated deeply enough to cover the crimping groove, and thus prevent any interference when chambering, it leaves enough room in the case for 56.0 grains of RS Pyrodex, the equivalent of a full 70-grain charge of FFG. Although this doesn't group as closely at 100 yards as I would like, I wouldn't hesitate a minute to take it deer hunting.

In the spring of 1986 I acquired a Navy Arms rolling block .45-70 with the intention of using it as a black powder rifle for testing cast bullets at long ranges. The rifle has a heavy 30-inch octagonal barrel $1\frac{1}{8}$ inches across flats with a bore that looks as perfect as they come. However, when I slugged the bore, I found that the groove diameter was .454 inch and the bore diameter was about .448 inch, far smaller than the average .45-70 barrel. Additionally, the chamber was a bit big and the freebore or throat was at least .459-inch in diameter.

Since I've always been under the impression that the bullet's diameter should match that of the throat for best accuracy, that is what I tried to use in the Navy Arms rolling block. When I first started out, I thought I had a real shooter in my hands. Then I found that the rifle was not consistent, that sometimes I would get a superb group and the very next group with the same identical load would scatter like a flock of chickens. It was so frustrating that I finally set the rifle aside with the intent to rebarrel.

Then along came Fred Cornell. Fred is a master craftsman on a machine whose abilities have splashed over into the muzzleloading game. Fred had built a .45-caliber slug rifle to be muzzleloaded with long, paper patched bullets weighing 550+ grains. To get these bullets, Fred made a swaging die for his heavy RCBS press.

There is no comparison between a swaged bullet and a cast bullet. The swaged bullet is smoother, denser and more uniform dimensionally. When Fred came to the house one evening with a double handful of swaged bullets, I felt like my cast bullets were on a par with a Model T Ford — good bullets, but 60 years behind the times.

Fred's unpatched bullets measured .443-inch. Wrapped with a nine-pound onionskin, they came up to about .451-inch, making them just right for loading down the muzzle of his slug gun and my Navy Arms rolling block!

Because of the freebored chamber, muzzleloading the rolling block proved to be a problem. To keep the base of the bullet ahead of the freebore, or flush with the origin of the rifling, and to ensure there was no air space between the powder and the base of the bullet, I had to insert a primed case in the chamber, pour enough powder down the muzzle to fill the case and the freebore, and then seat the bullet.

Such a practice is downright dangerous! It was totally different than loading a cap and ball rifle where a live primer or percussion cap doesn't go into position until everything else is done. To minimize the danger of such a practice, I placed a .177-inch thick steel ring over the hammer's nose and then let the hammer down against the breechblock. Thus the solid ring was held captive and could not drop out, while the hammer was held away from the firing pin with far more security than that offered by the half-cock notch.

For my first few shots loaded in this fashion, I used 80 grains of CTG Pyrodex and a 550-grain paper patched bullet. On every shot, the patch was stripped from the bullet and the bore was leaded. The CTG Pyrodex just would not hit the heavy pure lead bullet hard enough to slug it up in the bore even though the bullet was already a snug fit.

Since Fred was using 90 grains (weighed) of FFFg behind the same bullet in the slug rifle, I tried the same load in the rolling block. It shot and shot good, leading me to believe that a smaller diameter bullet (one that fitted the groove diameter instead of the throat diameter) in fixed ammunition just might give me the accuracy for which I had been looking.

To put this to the test, I cast a few very soft bullets from my Lyman 457132 Postell mould that had been shortened by one driving band. Originally this bullet was designed for use with black powder. It had a .444-inch diameter nose and weighed 475 grains. After running the bullets through my SAECO .458-inch die and filling the grooves with HVR lube, they were pushed nose first through the Corbin reducing die where they came out an even .452-inch.

The first five of these bullets were loaded in front of 54.0 grains of RS Pyrodex and fired at 50 yards, making a single ragged hole in the target about the size of a quarter. The remaining bullets were fired at 100 yards.

Due to a severe crosswind, I waited for a lull to fire the first two shots, and then said to hell with it and fired the last three. After looking at the target, I wished I had waited for a lull with all of the shots. Two shots were about an inch apart to the right, and the other three shots were crowded into one inch a bit to the left. Vertical dispersion was about half an inch.

Now it takes a whole lot more than a few shots to prove a rifle and/or load, and after the problems I had had with that rifle, I was more than reluctant to admit success even though things looked favorable. More bullets were cast and more groups were fired, some that looked fair and some not so fair. With fixed ammunition, the rifle just doesn't perform as it should.

Over the past 15 years I have fired well over 10,000 rounds of .45-70 ammunition in loads all the way from a light bullet at 450 fps to bullets and loads so heavy they made my teeth rattle. I've paper patched the Postell bullet and smoked it out the barrel on a rocket-size charge of IMR-4064, and I have used almost a full 20-pound keg of IMR-3031 making up standard hunting loads of 53.0 grains of IMR-3031 behind a 400-grain bullet, a combination that is tough to beat. Although a good .45-70 won't do all the things my .375 H&H rifles would do, for close-up smash in thick brushy areas it is a pretty tough cartridge to beat.

My first .45-70, a Winchester 1886 with a new barrel by Parker O. Ackley.

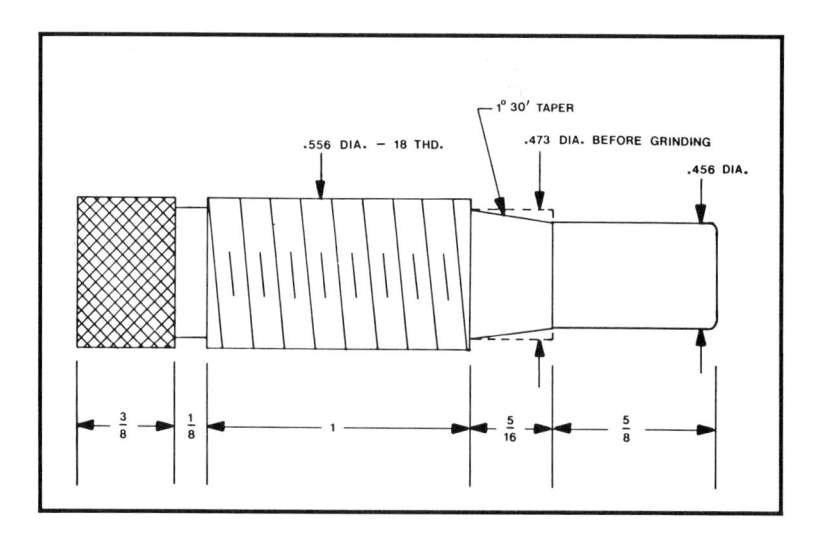

The neck expanding plug from an RCBS die modified as indicated to gently flare the case mouth prior to seating cast or paper patched bullets.

The Marlin 1895SS .45-70 equipped with a Lyman 66 receiver sight, a first class, big-bore repeating rifle.

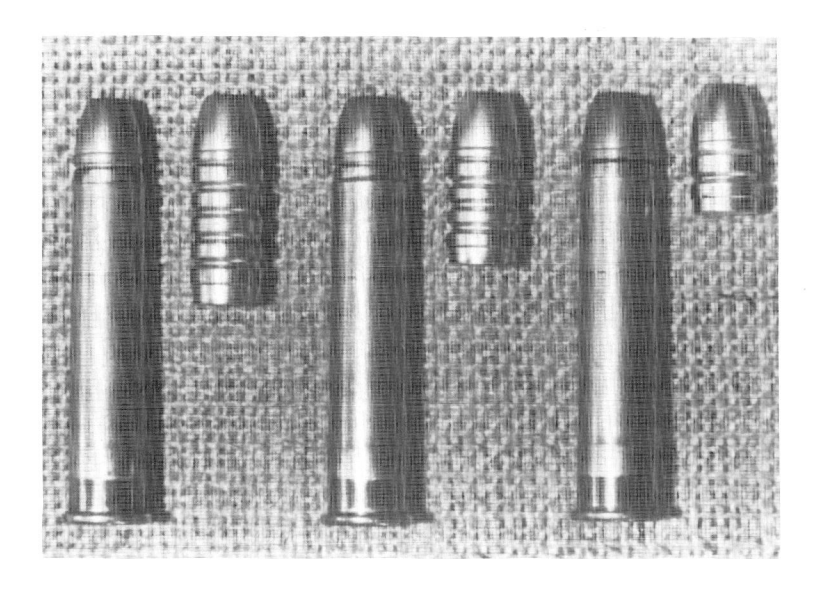

The three RCBS bullets designed for use in the Marlin rifle. As shown here the bullets are seated out for use in the Ruger single shot. For use in the Marlin, the bullets must be seated to the crimping groove.

Testing the Marlin off the bench. In this photo I was using my old KV scope purchased in 1952. Since then, a new Bushnell 2½x Banner scope has been installed. When testing rifles with heavy recoil, it helps to have a firm grip on the forearm.

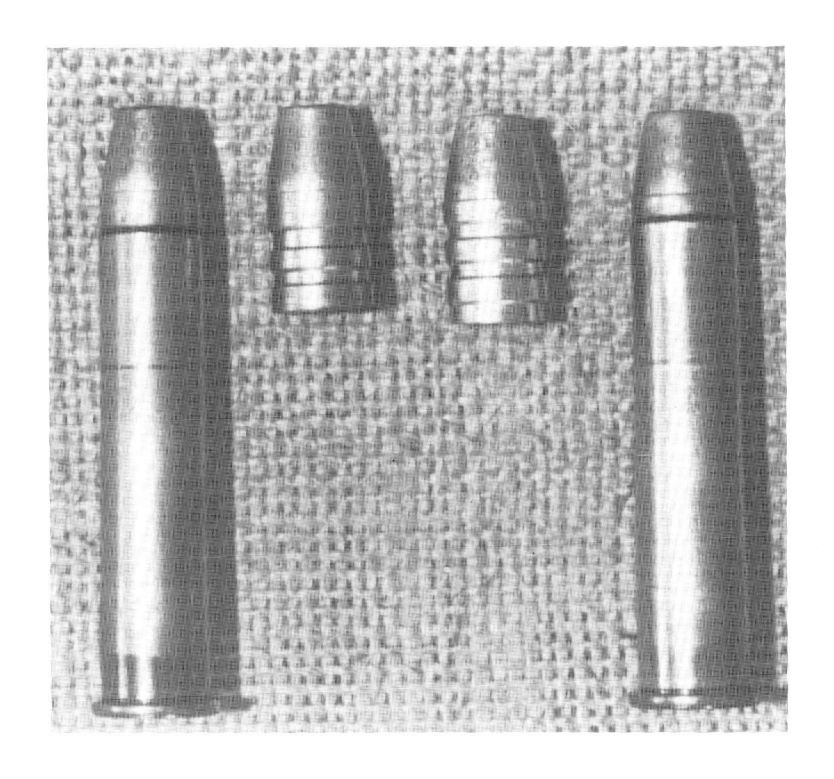

Two .45-70 cartridges and bullets from nose-pour moulds cut by Richard Hoch. Both bullets weigh about 355 grains when cast with a 75/25 mixture of wheelweights and lead.

Fred Cornell at the shooting bench with the .45-caliber slug gun he built. This rifle has a 36-inch barrel, 1⅛ inches across flats, with a false muzzle by Les Bauska of Kalispell, Montana. It has a 22-inch twist with a groove diameter of .458 and a bore diameter of .451 inch. When equipped with the 20x Unertl scope (as shown here), the rifle weighs 17½ pounds. Fred built this rifle so that it can be quickly converted to a .50-caliber roundball barrel with a 66-inch twist. With the roundball barrel and tang sight, the rifle weighs 14 pounds.

Checking the exit wound made by a .45-70 paper patched bullet on a wild hog. If you really want to know bullets, start sectioning them with a hacksaw and file, and then follow up by pawing around inside the game. Finish up with a close examination of entrance and exit wounds.

10

A .348 Winchester

One day back in 1952 I walked into the local hardware store and saw a Winchester Model 71 .348 in the rack. As the old-timers would say, I hefted it and it felt good. It pointed where I looked, the action was a modern clone of the old 1886 and the cartridge was a real bone smasher. To make things convenient for a trade, Betty had complained that the bolt action Arisaka 6.5x.257 was too clumsy and awkward for her. She was left-eyed and had to shoot from the left shoulder.

Now since the 6.5x.257 was a wildcat cartridge and the home-modified stock on the Arisaka wasn't any great thing of beauty, the hardware salesman wasn't all that keen about a swap. However, there was a dentist in town who was known to have his weaker moments whenever a rifle was involved, and so between the three of us I acquired the .348, the dentist got the 6.5x.257 and the hardware salesman got a fistful of dollars. We were all happy.

Make no mistake about it, the .348 was a powerhouse. It was also — in my opinion — a poorly designed cartridge with entirely too much body taper and a bastard-sized bullet. Why Winchester ever selected a .348-inch diameter bullet instead of a .358 or .375, I'll never know. Of course, hindsight is always 20/20 while foresight usually is lousy. In the .348 cartridge case and the strong, smooth-operating 71 action, Winchester had at their disposal the makings of a complete line of powerful proprietary cartridges that could encompass all calibers from the .358 to the .508. The lever action was still popular and the 71 was smoother to operate and easier to carry than the old 1895 with its protruding box magazine at the balance point. More than that, Africa, India, Canada and Alaska were still abundant with game — big game that took a lot of smash to put it down.

On the debit side, we as a nation were reeling against the ropes as a result of the Great Depression; bolt actions and high velocity were swiftly gaining popularity, and war clouds were hovering over Europe. Still, the .348 case on the Model 71 action had a lot of potential as evidenced by the fact that even today, there are those who will pay a good price to have a 71 rebored and rechambered to the .450 Alaskan or, on occasion, the mighty .500 Alaskan. On top of all this, Browning has re-introduced the great 71.

I was not particularly fond of the .348 cartridge. Although it had a lot of smash for woods hunting, a fairly good velocity to reduce the lead on running game and was plenty accurate for the first three or four shots before the barrel heated, the cartridge itself had too much body taper. The brass stretched badly, requiring that it be trimmed at almost every firing, and it had to exert too much back thrust on the breechblock. Add a bastard-sized bullet to this and you had a cartridge that was difficult to reload with few cast and jacketed bullets to select from.

As a rock smasher, the .348 would put on a spectacular display of turning rocks into dust. I used to take the rifle into the creekbed where I would set up stones the size of a dinner plate and two inches thick and smash them with a single 250-grain Silvertip.

One time I hung a ⅝-inch thick steel plate on the old chestnut and whaled away at it offhand at 50 yards. One shot was enough. Even before the recoil took the rifle off the target, I saw something hit the grass about 10 feet ahead of me. Walking over I picked up the still-hot bullet that had turned itself inside out and bounded back in a straight line.

Although we never shot anything with the .348, Betty carried it deer hunting one season before switching to the Model 1886 .45-70 which we both liked better. Somewhere along the line I purchased Lyman mould No. 350447, the one and only Lyman bullet available for the .348, and did some shooting with it. I've long forgotten what load I used, but whatever it was, I wasn't too impressed and the .348 was traded off.

11

The Model 92 .25-20

At the same time that I had the Winchester 1886 and 71, I purchased a Model 92 with 26-inch barrel and full-length magazine chambered for the .25-20. Turkeys were making a comeback in Pennsylvania and I figured the .25-20 would be a superb cartridge for the job.

Since the barrel had a few minor pits which could have put a damper on cast bullet performance, Charlie Canoll obtained a new barrel from Winchester — a 20-inch barrel, as I recall. The new barrel was installed and the magazine cut back to half-length. With a Lyman tang sight and a fine bead front, the rifle was almost perfect for small game and turkeys. Indeed, the previous owner's wife had shot three or four deer with it.

From Charlie, I borrowed a .25-caliber bullet mould casting an 85-grain plain base bullet, and a Lyman 310 nutcracker tool for reloading purposes. Perhaps because of the diminutive size of the cartridge or because it wasn't all that accurate, I never became enthused about the rifle. I shot a couple of porcupines and gray squirrels with it, but even at that, the rifle and cartridge didn't show me anything spectacular. If I was going to buy one of the new Marlin 1894 rifles today (and I just might do that!) it would be for the .32-20, not the .25-20.

I kept the .25-20 for three or four years, finally trading it in at the local hardware store for a brand new Ruger Blackhawk .357 Magnum, serial 653.

12

A Husqvarna .243

I was never a handgunner. For some reason handguns never impressed me as a precision weapon either for personal defense or hunting. I've never seen anything I could do with a handgun I couldn't do about 400 percent better with a rifle, except put it in my pocket. So after owning and using the Ruger Blackhawk for about five years, I was quick to trade it even up for a beautiful Husqvarna .243 with a Mannlicher stock and cheek rest. The rifle was equipped with a Lyman 48 receiver sight and bead front, and was a pleasure to carry. It also had a .30-06 length magazine and was throated so that I could seat the long 100-grain roundnose Hornady bullets well out preventing the base of the bullet from protruding into the powder chamber.

For quite a few years I used the rifle with its iron sights, shooting woodchucks and punching holes in paper. At 100 yards I usually could stay inside of 2½ inches, and I seldom missed a woodchuck at that range. There came a time, however, when I wanted to see what the rifle would really do, so I purchased and mounted a Weaver K6 scope. That was when I found out that I was shooting as good as the rifle would shoot, even with iron sights.

I've had very few rifles in my life that I couldn't make shoot the way I wanted. The Husqvarna was one of them. It made no difference what load, bullet or powder I used, a 2½ inch group was the best I could get. If I had never put the scope on the rifle, I would have been happy with it, but I figured if I could do 2½ inches with iron sights, I certainly ought to do less than an inch with a 6x scope!

Quite possibly the Mannlicher stock was to blame. I don't know. I've never tuned a rifle in my life because I'm a butcher when it comes to wood, and I don't have the equipment or knowhow to do metal work.

Had I considered the .243 a suitable deer cartridge, the little Husqvarna with its iron sights would have been as sweet a rifle to carry as one could desire but despite all the ballyhoo in favor of the 6mms as superb deer cartridges, with the .243 leading the pack, I've never been convinced. Quite to the contrary, I've known numerous men who swore by the .243 and killed any number of deer with it to prove their point. By the same token, these same men encountered many strange "misses" where the deer stood broadside for the shot and made a hasty departure afterward. They never could figure out how they missed such a shot, and I never could convince them that they probably didn't miss, but hit a heavy shoulder bone instead of slipping the bullet between the ribs so that it could get inside to do its work

Just this past November a friend of mine came to the house to sight in his .243 for the upcoming season and as always he kidded me about my reservations on the cartridge.

"Someday," I told him, "you're going to have a calendar picture shot at a prize buck, and when you're finished, he's going to thumb his nose at you and take off!"

I didn't know at the time just how prophetic my words were, but that was precisely what happened and another party finally killed the buck. John had hit it exactly where he wanted, but the fragile .243 bullet just didn't have enough heft to do the job. Two weeks later John made a repeat performance on a big doe, and another man finally killed that animal.

Now I don't mind missing a deer as I've missed my share and maybe more, but by the Great Jehovah and the First Continental Congress, when I hit a deer where I'm aiming, I want the animal down right then — not three hours and four miles later with no blood trail to follow! I had enough of that with the '06 and 150-grain bronzepoint bullets to last me a lifetime. I don't need to go asking for it.

The .243 is a fine cartridge and may prove to be the berries for antelope and for deer in some of our southern and southwestern states where I believe deer are considerably smaller than here in Pennsylvania. Indeed, just yesterday I looked at a picture of a six-point buck killed in Texas that field dressed 88 pounds. I doubt there is a six-point buck in the whole of Pennsylvania that will field dress less than 115 pounds, and I've seen deer that went 186 pounds field dressed.

Still, the .243 is a very popular cartridge in some areas, and popularity usually is based on some degree of success. For me, however, I've seen and heard too much evidence of high-velocity light bullet failure on deer that were psyched up on fear and overdosed with adrenalin. So with no regrets, the little .243 Husqvarna went the way of the .348 and the .25-20.

13

The .458

Every rifleman should own at least one true big bore rifle, a rifle that takes a case at least 2¼ inches long and has a hole down the snout that will accept a .40-caliber or larger bullet weighing at least 330 grains. Preferably it should be a rimmed cartridge dating back to the black powder era of buffalo and ivory, but as long as it meets the physical criteria stated above, we'll go for it.

No man has to have real justification for such a rifle — just wanting one is enough. So when my nephew, Joe Piccolo, approached me about my pre-64 Winchester Model 70 .375 H&H, I told him to buy me a new Ruger No. 1 .458 and the Model 70 was his.

Now I had really had a hankering for a .458 for some time, but not because there was an elephant problem with the crops, or a bear getting into my beehives. I wanted a big bore, large-case-capacity single shot rifle that I could use with black powder and cast bullets. I wanted to be able to put a scope on the rifle without destroying its originality, and I wanted to be able to magnumize my loads if so desired. On top of that, I wanted a straight case.

If there is any one production rifle built and chambered for cast bullets, the Ruger No. 1 .458 Magnum is it. The chamber is cut in accordance with SAAMI specifications, which means that the throat is a long, gentle taper of less than half a degree beginning at the case mouth and extending up the bore for a bit more than one inch. Although this is done primarily to accommodate long, heavy jacketed bullets, it is a natural for paper patched bullets as well as the conventional cast bullet.

The chamber on my rifle was as perfect as I had ever had on any rifle, just large enough to let the case release the bullet. If I had any reservations about the quickness of the 14-inch twist and its ability to handle soft bullets, I forgot it at the first bench session.

The .458 case will hold 90 grains of FFg black powder and still leave room to seat a 565-grain paper patched bullet if a drop tube is used to settle the powder in the case. Right here, I should point out that with black powder a drop tube is the only way to go. Although you can compress Pyrodex — and I found it necessary to do so in the .45-70 case — compressing black powder has a tendency to break up the powder kernels, thus actually changing the burning rate. My experience with Pyrodex is that the kernels might be reshaped a bit by compression, but they do not break or fracture so as to change the amount of burning surface.

Because of the fact that black powder fouling in the throat interfered when chambering a cartridge, and I hadn't yet learned to reduce the bullet's size by running it through my Corbin reducing die, I used a duplex load of 12.0 grains of SR-4759 next to the primer and 76.0 grains of GOEX FFg black powder on top. This was capped off with a 490-grain paper patched bullet for my Hoch mould, giving me a cartridge that I would have been proud to show any buffalo hunter of the 1870s.

Since one grain of SR-4759 is the equivalent of three grains of black, the load I was using was comparable to 112 grains of FFg. When clocked over the Oehler 33D Chronotach, the velocity averaged 1,407 fps with a muzzle energy of 2,146 foot-pounds.

Although this bullet and load combination gave good accuracy and chambered without a hitch, I had less than

¼-inch of space in the case in which to seat the bullet, not nearly enough to firmly support the bullet if the cartridge is to be carried afield. Accordingly, I reduced the amount of black powder to 72.0 grains and increased the bullet weight to 550 grains in order to keep the leading edge of the patch close to the rifling.

Somewhere in the process of all this, I learned that the barrel of the .458 was tighter than those on my .45-70s, and that the .458 much preferred the .450-inch bullets from my Canoll mould as opposed to the .452-inch bullets from my Hoch mould. Although the difference in bullet diameter is slight, it made a significant difference on the target — five shots going into $1\frac{3}{8}$ inches at 100 yards with no cleaning between shots.

For statistics, the bullet is $1\frac{11}{32}$ inches long and wears a one-inch wide patch covering $\frac{11}{16}$ inch of the bullet. There is not enough overhang of the patch to twist into a tail, so it is tucked into the base cavity with a twisting motion to tighten the patch.

This makes a good black powder load similar to the old .45-100-550 cartridge. When I shot it, I knew I had an armful of rifle although the recoil was much more of a solid push than a smashing blow.

Hoping to work up a good express load akin to the old Winchester .45-125, I went back to 76.0 grains of FFg and 12.0 grains of SR-4759 with the short, stubby bullet from the RCBS 45-300-FN mould. The bullet was seated just deep enough to cover the grease grooves, but in that long-leade chamber it had to jump too far to engage the rifling. Accuracy was poor.

The RCBS 45-400-FN bullet over 60.0 grains of FFg and 10.0-grain priming charge of SR-4759 would stay close to two inches at 100 yards, but was not on a par with my heavy paper patched bullet. Recoil was considerably lighter and it would probably make a practical deer load.

Going to smokeless loads with cast bullets gave a feeling for the latent power of the .458. Even before I had the rifle in hand, I had cast some bullets from the RCBS 45-500-FN mould using a very soft alloy that on my LBT bullet hardness tester registered about 6 BHN. This was a bit harder than pure lead, but surely soft enough to guarantee expansion. The bullets weighed 530 grains.

Using fired, unsized cases, I regulated the load so that I would have 100 percent loading density when the bullet was seated to cover all of the grease grooves and crimped just enough to hold the bullet in the case. This amounted to 55.0 grains of IMR-4064.

At the time of the first firing, I had a Weaver K3 scope on the rifle, but after I put five shots into a 1¾ inches at 100 yards, I mounted a K6 and found that the rifle and load would shoot just about as close as I could hold.

Although this wasn't a full throttle .458 load, neither was it a piker. Over the Oehler Skyscreens it registered an average of 1,659 fps with 3,243 foot-pounds of muzzle energy! More than that, the load shot clean without a hint of leading in the barrel. The lubricant was Rooster Laboratories' SL4. Had I wanted, I probably could have boosted the velocity by 150 to 200 feet per second by switching to an equal charge of IMR-3031. I have no doubt that such a load would handle just about anything I would ever want to shoot with the .458.

Using the RCBS bullet doesn't give the cartridge the cigar-length appearance one usually associates with the big bores. As I mentioned earlier, all the weight is in the back end of the bullet in the form of driving bands and grease grooves, and is therefore seated out of sight in the case. Not so with my paper patched bullets.

Taking some of my 550-grain paper patched bullets from the Canoll mould, I loaded them on top of 78 grains of H-4831, again making certain I had 100 percent loading density. This load also gave good accuracy and had an average velocity of 1,686 fps with 3,443 foot-pounds of muzzle energy. The powder burned clean, but barely, indicating that maybe an equal charge of IMR-4350 would be better if I thought additional velocity was necessary.

One thing I have always found to be true with the straight cases such as the .45-70 and .458, is that a load having 100 percent loading density (i.e., the case is full to the base of the bullet) usually gives the best of everything in the velocity and accuracy departments. Obviously, the correct powder must be used, one that burns completely clean but not so fast that it wrecks the rifle and shooter. In fact, it doesn't hurt to use a powder a bit on the slow side, like the 78.0-grain load of H-4831. This leaves just a trace of unburnt kernels in the barrel telling me that pressures are moderate and well on the safe side. I could go to an equal charge of the fast-burning IMR-4350 and probably belt those heavy bullets out the muzzle close to 1,900 fps, but I really don't see the need when all I'm doing is punching paper and converting rocks to dust. If I was going to perforate a lion or go after buffalo or Kodiak bear, then I would up the charge for the occasion, but for now I'm having fun with my honest-to-God big bore rifle. Every rifleman should have one!

Two fine rifles, the Ruger No. 1 .458 Magnum on the left and the .45-70 on the right.

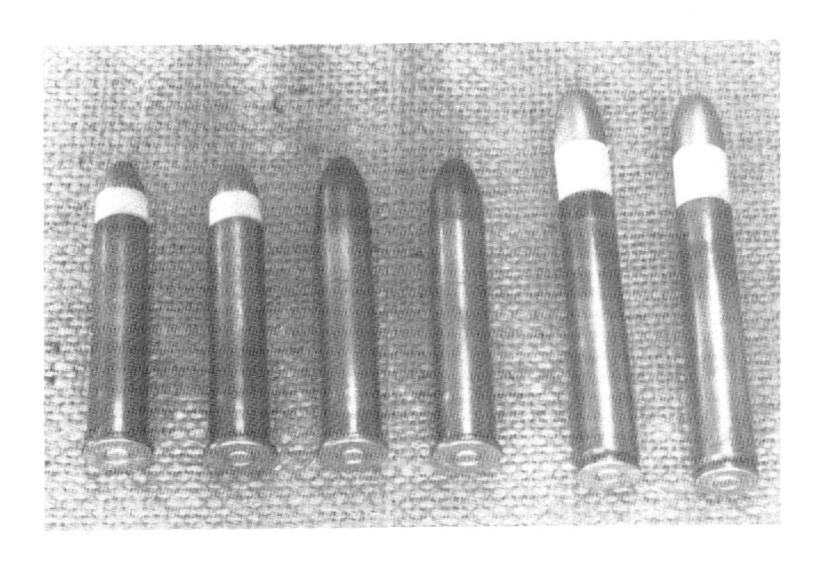

Four .45-70 and two .458 cartridges loaded with paper patched bullets. The black bullets in the center have been waterproofed and wiped with graphite. The .45-70 bullets weigh 400 grains, while the .458 bullets weigh 550 grains.

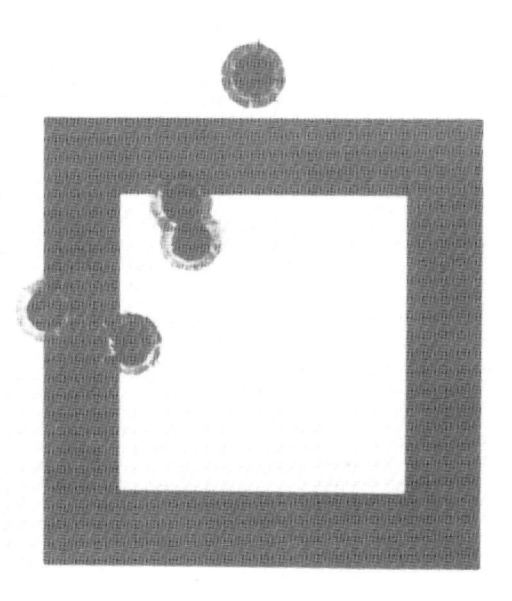

Accuracy of the cast bullet in the .458 Magnum. These bullets were very soft, about 6 or 7 BHN. Distance between centers is 2⅛ inches.

14

A New Model 1863 Sharps

In the afternoon of July 3, 1863, men in blue crouched behind a stone wall on the fields of Gettysburg. Their hearts pounded and their mouths grew dry as they watched the long gray ranks forming a mile away across a gentle valley. Sabers flashed in the sunlight as officers rode back and forth dressing the lines, and bayonets gleamed in a thick forest of cold steel.

Not a single man was present who didn't feel the tight knot of fear in his guts, and as the gray ranks started flowing, moving to left or right as necessary, the cannon on the hill behind the stone wall opened fire, first with shot, then cannister and then the deadly grape.

There is no glory in war. No man with a soul can stand on the Gettysburg battlefield today amidst the row upon row of white markers and not feel the tears come to his eyes. The Blue and the Gray, they met at Gettysburg.

Today there are many reenactments of those bygone battles by a devoted few who wear the dress of the period and who carry rifles and muskets of that time, either original or replica. Both men and women — these students of history make every attempt at historical accuracy.

Such was not the case back in the 1950s when a neighbor woman handed me a Sharps New Model 1863 in fairly good condition and remarked that her grandfather had brought it home from the Civil War. In those days the Civil War was history, not yet 100 years past, and the old units of both the North and South had yet to be reactivated. As I held that rifle in my hands and swung it to my shoulder to squint along the barrel, I could smell the brimstone of burnt powder, hear the rebel yell as the gray ranks advanced on the run, and feel the terror of those who had to face the points of gleaming bayonets. Like the men behind the wall at Gettysburg, I just had to shoot that old rifle.

Before continuing I must clear up a point or correct a mistake I made over 30 years ago. The serial number of the rifle in question was C,30303 and it was brought home from the war by Private Samuel H. Williams of Company C, 171st Pennsylvania Volunteers. When I wrote about this rifle in the *1957 Gun Digest*, I placed it at Gettysburg in order to give the article a bit of color and flavor. *But that particular rifle was not at Gettysburg. It had not even been built at the time of the Gettysburg battle.* In fact, I'm not certain that Company C of the 171st was at Gettysburg at the time of the battle, nor am I certain that it wasn't there!

I had to mention that because after the article was published under the name of "The Gettysburg Sharps," it seemed that everyone who owned a Sharps New Model 1863 rifle wrote to me. Some very knowledgeable gun collectors wanted to know if their rifle had been used at Gettysburg and if so how much it was worth. It was a mistake I don't care to repeat.

Although I'm not going to discuss the rifle's mechanics, I will say that even with its 30-inch barrel and weight of 8¾ pounds, the rifle balanced nicely, came up fast and hung steady. For the infantryman or for the post-war hunter, it was a pleasure to carry and use. Even the sights, although of the open variety with a thin blade up front and a V-leaf rear, were the best of the era. The trigger pull was a bit better than six pounds and by the time I got to shoot the rifle almost 90 years after it came home from the war, the barrel was pitted at the breech.

Private Williams' rifle had a bore diameter of .518 inch and a groove diameter of .529 inch, so I purchased Lyman mould No. 533476 casting a hollowbase Minie ball weighing 410 grains. I have long since forgotten what alloy was used, although I strongly suspect it was pure lead. The Minie balls were dipped into whatever concoction I was using as a lubricant at the time, and were then wrapped to make a paper cartridge.

The paper used for making the cartridges was a thin, hard tracing paper similar to nine-pound onionskin made of 100 percent cotton fiber. At least some of the paper used was nitrated by soaking it in a solution of saltpeter (potassium nitrate) and water. This was to ensure that it burned cleanly and didn't leave any glowing embers in the chamber. Whether I nitrated all the paper or not, I don't know, but since I didn't mention it in the *Gun Digest* article, I have to assume that most of my cartridges used plain, unnitrated paper.

To make my paper cartridges, I first got a steel dowel four inches long and .533 inch in diameter. Then taking a piece of paper four inches long and wide enough to go around the bullet twice, I wrapped it around the Minie ball and the dowel, just covering the grease grooves on the Minie ball. Using a small brush, the top edge of the paper was cemented to the Minie ball and the seam along the side was cemented with water glass. Water glass is a viscous mixture of water and sodium silicate and was once used quite widely in the country for preserving eggs. I believe it was also used on the outside of casts on broken limbs, and may still be available from the local drugstore.

The water glass dried almost immediately, firmly cementing the paper to the bullet and leaving a nice tube into which I poured 55.0 grains of DuPont Fg. The tail of the tube was then trimmed to length, pinched flat, folded up against the cartridge's body and cemented into place with water glass.

In use, the tail of the patch was pulled from the side of the cartridge as the cartridge was inserted into the chamber. Raising the breechblock sheared off the tail, exposing the powder to the hot Fiocchi musket caps then distributed by Alcan. These caps gave plenty of flame and never once misfired.

I knew very little about black powder shooting in those days, and I'm certain today that my lubricant left a lot to be desired. Even so, at 100 yards with pitted barrel, six-pound trigger and iron sights, that old rifle put 10 shots into a space that measured seven inches vertically by 5½ inches horizontally. Six of those 10 shots were inside of three inches!

Since there was considerable gas escapage around the breechblock of that old rifle, one shot with black powder would put enough fouling between the breechblock and the mortice in which it operated to freeze the block up solid. Greasing the face plate and the rear face of the barrel with tallow helped alleviate this to some degree, and a mixture of waterpump grease and graphite worked even better. I finally solved the problem by wiping a small gob of grease on the inside edge of the chamber before closing the breech. When the rifle was fired, the grease was blown out with the escaping gases and kept the fouling soft enough so that the action could be opened and closed.

I never shot anything with that Sharps, although I did go after woodchucks with it a few times before returning it to its owner. The owner's husband remarked to me many times about how he would like to use it on deer, and there is little doubt in my mind that the 410-grain Minie ball would do an efficient job. It certainly proved its capability on the fields at Gettysburg.

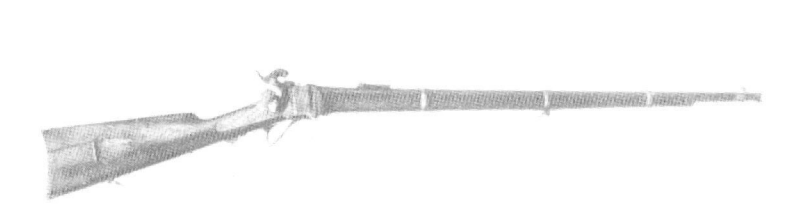

The New Model 1863 Sharps, serial C,30303.

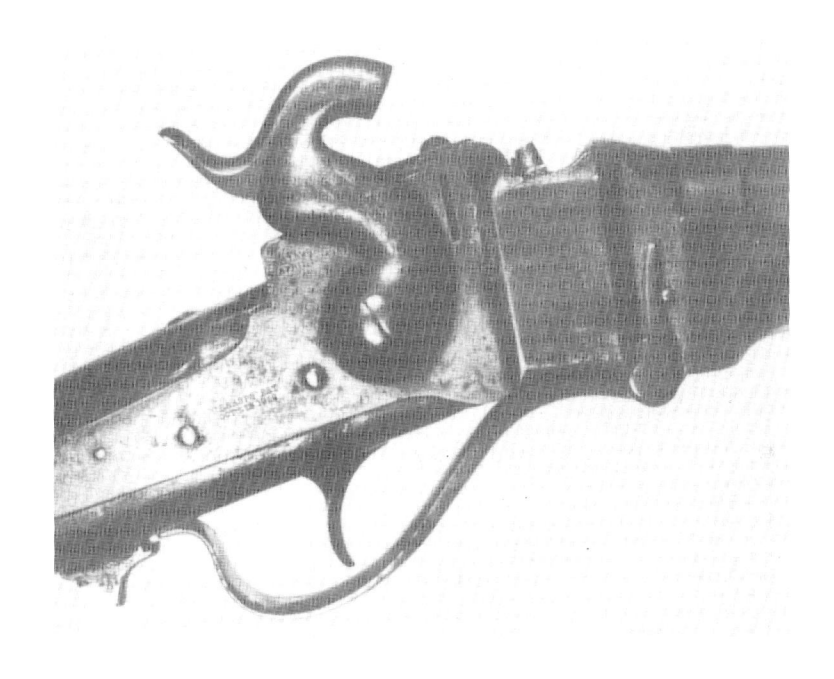

Close-up of the Sharps percussion action.

Rolling the paper cartridge.

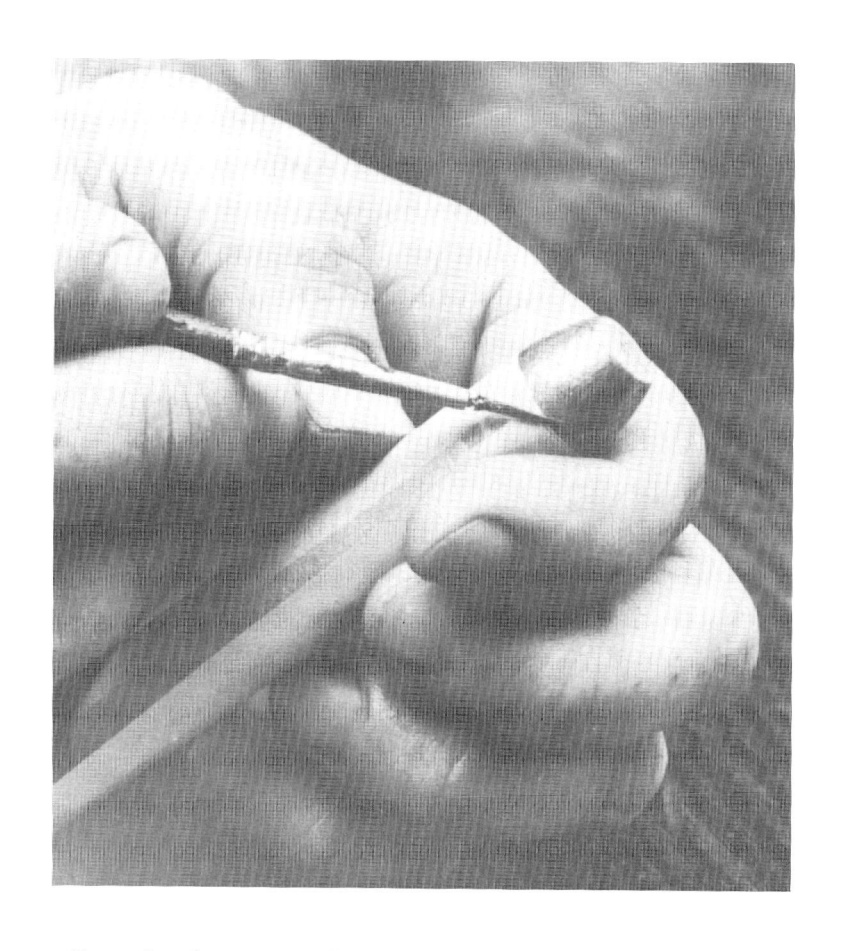

Cementing the paper to the bullet with water glass.

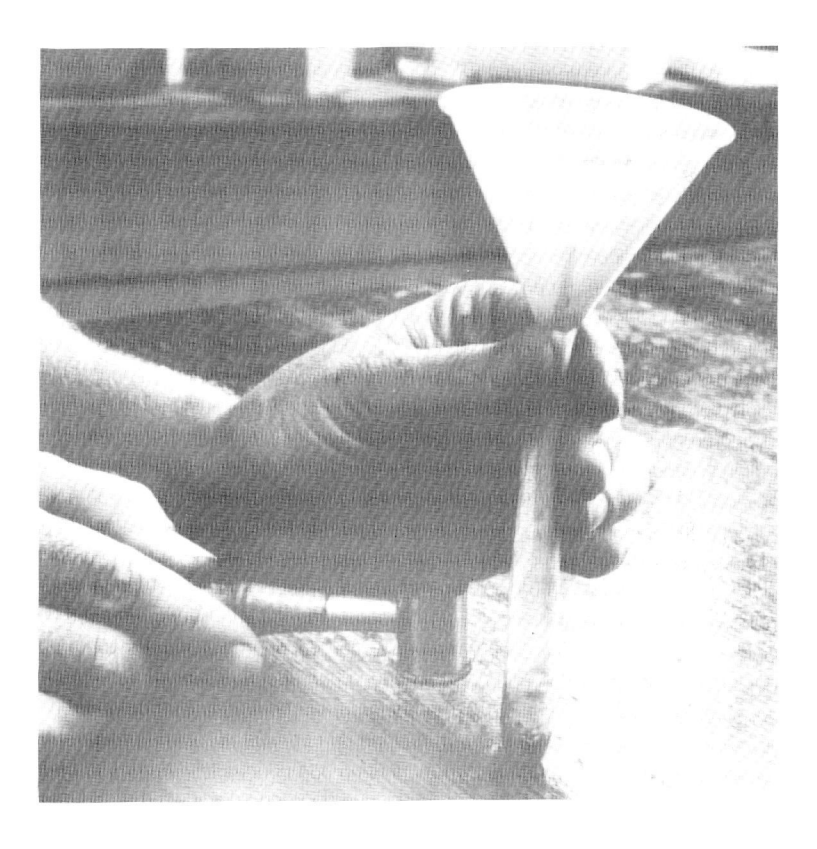

Filling the tube with 55.0 grains of DuPont Fg.

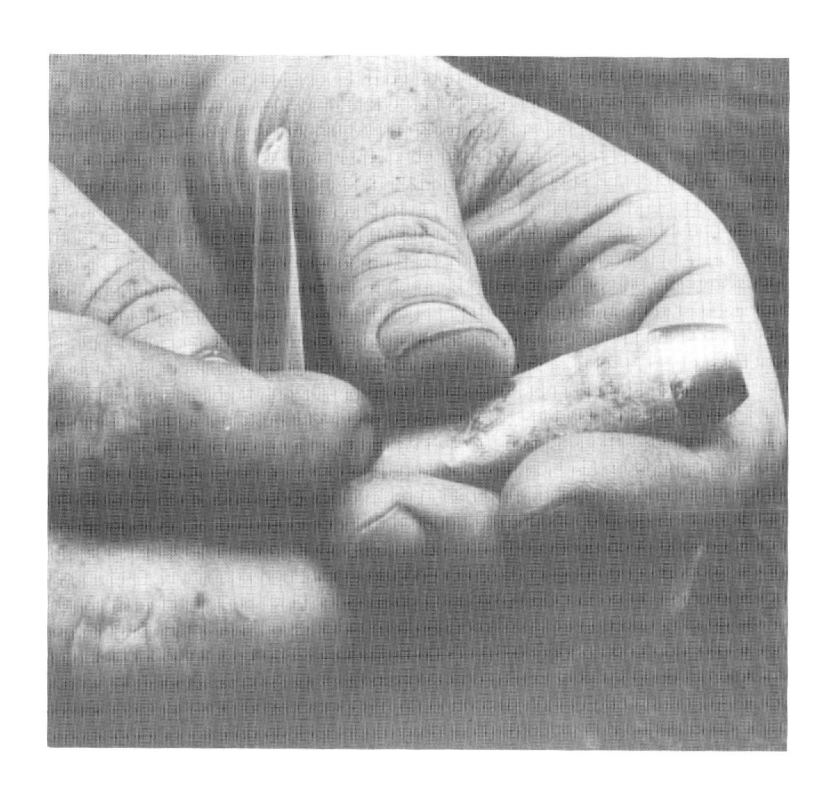

Bending the flattened tail.

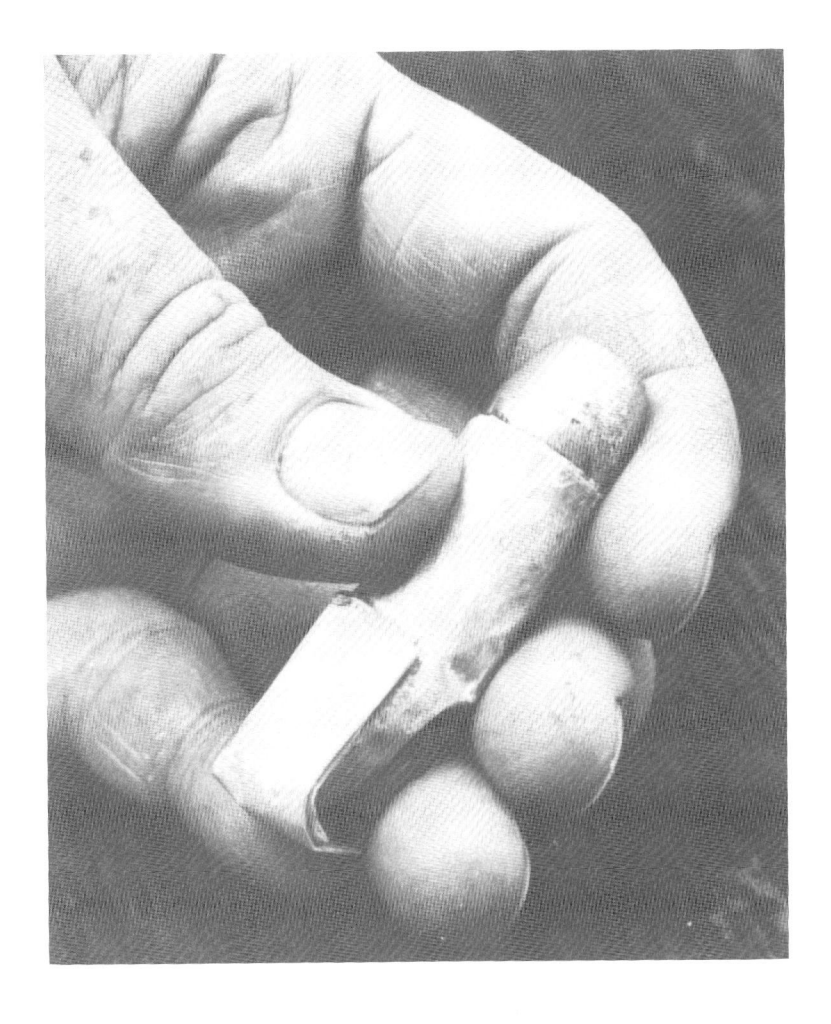

The finished cartridge with the tail trimmed and cemented.

15

The Lyman Great Plains Rifle

Whether it was intuition or some slight sound, I'll never know, but when I turned around, there was the doe walking at a determined gait as though she had a specific place in mind and specific time to be there. Without even thinking, my thumb curled around the cock and as I heard it slip into the full-cock notch my finger set the trigger and the sharply curved butt of the Lyman Great Plains Rifle snuggled against my coat.

Swinging ahead of the doe, the muzzle of the rifle sought an open spot through the brush, reaching it just in time for the sights to come into alignment high over the doe's foreleg. My finger caressed the trigger, the powder in the pan spit fire and the deep bellow of a full charge of FFg roared out across the land, echoing and reverberating in the ravines and hollows that fingered downward into Goose Hollow.

The 410-grain Minie ball struck the doe at the point of aim, spinning her completely around before collapsing onto the winter frozen leaves. The range was 47 long paces, and even before I reached her, she was dead — dead as quickly and efficiently as though I had used one of the new short-necked magnums.

Although I had fought it for a long time, I knew that eventually I would go to a front stuffer, and I knew that when I did, it would be a .54-caliber for two different reasons.

First, when using a roundball rifle, the only thing going for you is weight and diameter. Velocity is about the same regardless of caliber, 1,300 to 1,400 fps out where the game is. The large ball punches a bigger hole and has a lot more weight to help in the penetration department. It's as simple as that.

Secondly, I still had the Minie ball mould used with the 1863 Sharps. Cast of pure lead it measured .533-inch in diameter, and when patched with a nine-pound onionskin it made a thumb-push fit in the muzzle of a clean .54-caliber barrel.

The Lyman Great Plains Rifle has a 66-inch twist which is just great for a roundball but a shade too slow for the Minie ball or any of its modern counterparts. Even so, at 50 yards off the bench using coarse iron sights, I could keep the heavy slug inside three inches when backed with a stout load of GOEX FFg.

That the Minie ball was a killer, there is no doubt. It went in one side of my large doe and out the other to keep on whistling through the trees and brush to God knows where. Its devastation inside the animal was equal to that of any cartridge rifle I had ever used and, as far as a flintlock is concerned, far more powerful than necessary. Further, the pressures with the Minie ball were far greater than with a roundball when using the same charge, and the Minie ball shot low and to the right of the roundball. So after using the paper patched Minie ball for that first deer, I went to the patched roundball and have used it ever since. (Pennsylvania game law now requires a cloth-patched roundball be used during the muzzleloading season.)

When it comes to cloth-patched roundballs, there are an infinite number of combinations one can come up with involving ball diameter, patch thickness and patch lube. Without exploring the details of several months of experimentation to find the right combination for my rifle, let me say that going from a .530-inch roundball to a .535-inch roundball made a significant improvement in accuracy, whereas going to a thicker patch with the smaller diameter ball accomplished no improvement whatsoever. My patch and ball combination for now and evermore is a .535-inch pure lead ball wrapped in a .017-inch pillow ticking patch.

As far as patch lubes are concerned, I ran the gauntlet on that, too. For informal shooting and target practice, it's difficult to beat one of the fluid patch lubes like Rooster Laboratories' Rooster Pop. This thick, white fluid has the consistency of mucilage, and saturating the patch with it permits shot after shot without having to clean the bore. However, since it's a liquid lube, you cannot leave the barrel loaded for any length of time without contaminating the powder.

For hunting purposes, I use Rooster Laboratories' Minie Lube on my patches. This is a grease/wax lube that remains soft and pliable, but which doesn't migrate into the powder even if the rifle is left loaded for several days. When using it, I put a thick coat of it on one side of the patch — the side that goes down bore — rubbing some of it into the fabric.

I lube only one side of the patch because when the ball and patch exit the muzzle, I don't want anything on the patch that might give it a tendency to stick to the ball. A cloth patch sticking to the ball for an instant before dropping free would have about the same effect as part of a paper patch clinging to a bullet or the old style gas checks that might or might not cling to the bullet's shank. Inconsistency begets inconsistency, and uniformity begets uniformity, and it makes little difference whether you're breeding cattle, baking cakes or loading ammunition!

For a long time while I was using Crisco-thin lubes, I had a problem of my patches burning through when using heavy hunting loads. Naturally, when this happens accuracy is a sometimes thing with the sometimes quite far apart. After I started using a heavy coating of Minie Lube on the patch, my burned-through patches disappeared.

Another lube that performs as well as the Minie Lube is the mixture of beeswax and Vaseline™ that I use on my paper patched bullets. I've used both lubes with heavy loads and see no difference. With respect to these lubes, I should also mention that while I have reloaded without cleaning the bore between shots, it is far more difficult than when using the fluid patch lube. Moreover, I am a firm believer in cleaning after every shot even when I'm in the woods hunting deer.

I must confess that even though I love hunting with a flintlock, even rate it far above that of a cartridge rifle, I have no desire to don buckskins, beads, moccasins and coonskin hat and play at being Lew Wetzel. I have nothing against the practice either, but am a practical man with practical objectives.

I bring this up because there are those of us who refuse to break from tradition in any respect. There are some who refuse to use any patch except those cut at the muzzle, and for a long time I spent hours with my wife's sewing shears cutting out 1¼-inch round patches. Then I discovered that a 1¼-inch square patch worked just as well and could be produced in about one-tenth of the time. That's what I use today.

When I first got my Lyman Great Plains Rifle, I was disappointed at the load recommendations given by the manufacturer — 80 grains of FFFg or 100 grains of FFg with a roundball. The FFFg load gives an average velocity of 1,483 fps from my rifle, while the FFg load is probably about 1,550 fps though I never checked it across the Skyscreens.

Both loads seem quite anemic when you consider that with a heavy-barreled, .54-caliber, muzzle velocity could easily be in the 1,900 to 2,000 fps bracket if a heavy charge of powder is used.

However, the barrel on the Great Plains rifle is only $^{15}/_{16}$-inch across flats, making it a rather thin-walled barrel when bored for .54-caliber. More than that, for any given velocity with a given ball size, pressures with FFFg powder are considerably higher than with FFg. The 80-grain load of FFFg makes an easy shooting, accurate target load with quite a few shots per pound. That's what I use it for and I don't exceed the 80-grain charge.

Although I believe that the manufacturers' loading recommendations are on the conservative side as protection against product liability suits, I also must say that the thin-walled barrel doesn't leave much margin for error, especially in short-seating a ball.

From what I have read, almost every burst barrel on a muzzleloader can be traced to a short-seated ball, and from personal experience, short-seating is something that can happen all too easily. I almost did it twice in the same day.

When I reload ammunition for a cartridge rifle, I make every attempt to be alone at the time so that I am not distracted, but loading a muzzleloader is an entirely different ball game. Usually I'm shooting at the gong or target and am in the company of someone else. Conversation flows back and forth in a steady stream. Quite often I'm asked a question just at the time I've started a ball down the barrel and I'll stop to think or make a reply and forget all about ramming the ball home.

I did this twice one day while Charlie Canoll and I were in the process of chronographing, and each time Charlie reminded me that the ball hadn't been fully seated. Would the barrel have burst had I fired with the short-seated ball? I don't know, but I believe it certainly would have had a walnut in it. With a heavy load in excess of the manufacturer's recommendation, I believe it would have come apart.

So although the manufacturer's recommended load for a given muzzleloader may seem on the mild side, it isn't a bad idea to follow those recommendations. Unless there is an overabundance of luck on the premises, when a muzzleloader comes apart someone is going to get hurt.

It took me three or four years of hunting with the flintlock to learn the finer points of convenience, speed of loading, positive ignition and as little equipment as possible.

Each man probably has his own idea of how it all should be done and I'm certain these ideas will vary, but this is the way I do it:

In my leather hunting pouch, I carry six premeasured charges of powder and 10 to 12 balls. In a small tin container, I carry 10 prelubed patches stuck together face-to-face with the lube. For cleaning the rifle between shots, I take a stack of 10 cleaning patches saturated, but not dripping, with moose milk — a 50/50 mixture of water and a water-soluble oil — and put these in a Ziploc™ bag in the pouch. In another Ziploc™ bag I carry 10 dry flannel patches. I also carry a cleaning jag, ball puller, patch retriever, wire pick, short starter and a spare flint. I always start with a new flint in the rifle.

Before leaving the house in the morning, I wipe the barrel free of all oil, using two or three dry flannel patches. I check the opening in the touchhole liner with the pick, and then I put a charge down the barrel while leaning the rifle to one side so that the powder will enter the recess on the inside of the touchhole liner. This puts my main charge of powder within $\frac{1}{16}$ inch of the pan and almost guarantees positive and instant ignition. A patched ball is then rammed home, seated firmly on the powder.

To me it is important to lean the rifle so that powder will enter the recess in the touchhole liner. Without leaning the rifle, it often happens that the powder stacks and packs so tightly in the chamber that even smacking the butt half a dozen times will not jar the powder into the liner recess, but leaves it a full half-inch from the pan.

When I return home or to camp that night, if I haven't fired the rifle, I usually stick a round toothpick in the touchhole and leave the rifle outside for the night. Bringing a cold rifle in the house causes moisture to condense on the cold metal, possibly within the chamber of the barrel where it could contaminate the powder. If I've shot the rifle during the day, then it has to be given a thorough cleaning.

Instead of carrying loose patches and balls, some hunters like to use a loading block having six or eight holes with each hole containing a patched ball. My brother Ernie uses a loading block. His rifle is identical to mine and he made his loading block so that it would slide down over the barrel's muzzle, aligning the patched ball with the bore. This works for him and there is little question that it is faster than loose balls and patches.

Just as with any other rifle, the flintlock requires a lot of practice. After shooting two deer in a row with mine, I got kind of cocky and figured that offhand practice with the .45-70 all summer made practice with the flintlock unnecessary. Not so. The ignition and barrel time with the flintlock is much slower than that of the cartridge rifle and requires a significant follow-through.

After killing my second deer with the flintlock, I missed the next three with no justifiable excuse for any of them. Every shot was a clean broadside shot and should have put meat in the freezer. The only reason it didn't was because I hadn't practiced enough.

Two of the deer, shot at only one day apart, were missed because I had changed the rear sight on the rifle and figured I had sighted it in after a single session at the bench. Then I changed the size of the ball from .530 to .535 inch and I changed the load. After missing the two deer, I took a half day off from hunting to determine that my shots had gone eight inches high. I filed the rear sight down to where it belonged.

The miss on the third deer was simply because I hurried the shot and went too high, a bad habit for which there is no excuse and which only practice will correct — offhand practice at a gong, not over sandbags off the bench which only tests the rifle.

Don't think for a minute that the man who hunts with a muzzleloader, especially a large caliber, is undergunned — he isn't. At 50 yards that soft 225-grain, .54-caliber ball will sail crosswise through a deer, smashing bones as it goes, and keep right on going. The 50-yard energy figures on a piece of paper may only be in the three digits, but kinetic energy is no more a yardstick of killing power today than it was when they decimated the buffalo with black powder and pig lead over 100 years ago. I have been told (and I cannot verify the accuracy of this statement) that the kinetic energy figures came into use when Winchester introduced the .30-30 and had to find some way of showing it to be more powerful than the .45-70.

There is nothing quite like taking your deer or other game with a flintlock. It's like reaching back 200 years to shake hands with some grizzled old woodsman who stalked the eastern frontier from Niagara to Fort Pitt, who trod the virgin forests of Pennsylvania (then known as The Shades of Death) from Danbury, Connecticut, to the confluence of the Susquehanna and Chemung rivers in northern Pennsylvania. Using a flintlock is like reliving a piece of history, a history that all too many people today are willing to forget.

The Lyman .54 caliber Great Plains flintlock rifle.

Cutting 1¼-inch patches for the flintlock. Square patches work equally well.

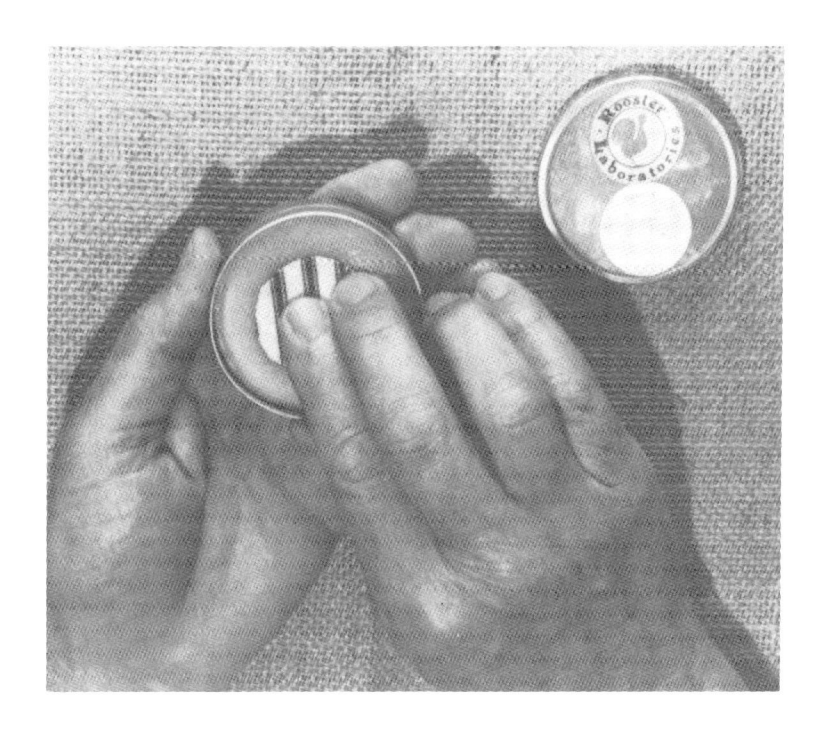

Lubricating one side of the patch with Minie Lube.

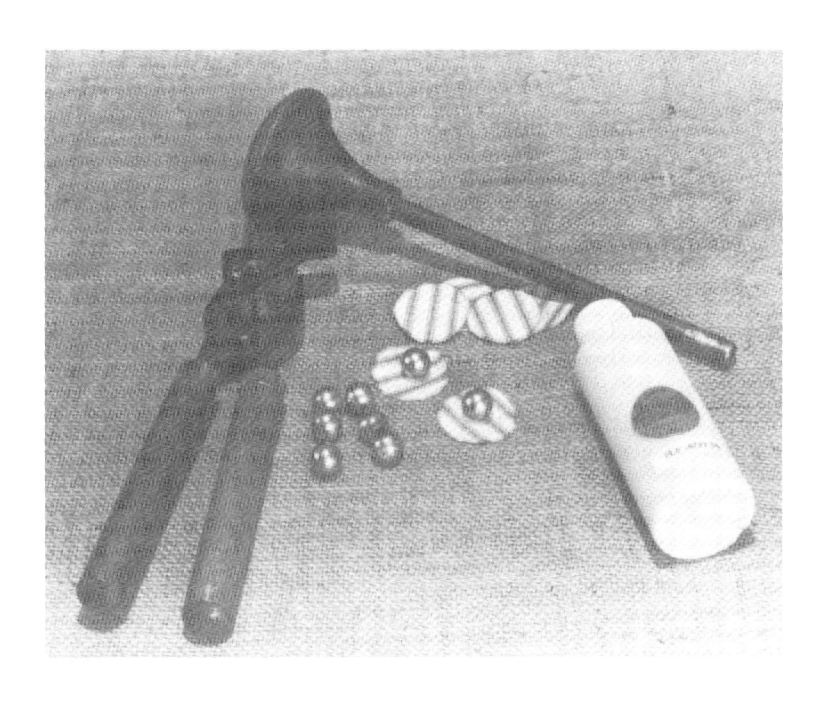

Lee ball mould, .535-inch roundballs, patches, liquid lube and starter.

16

Odds and Ends

Riflemen come in all shapes and sizes, and each has a different idea of what he expects from a rifle. I am a practical man. I was raised during the Great Depression when we learned to make do with what we had and to improve upon it if possible. The important thing, however, was to get the job done in such a fashion that there was no question about whether or not it was done or how well it was done.

That's the way I am with a rifle. I want a rifle that I can carry hunting, not a rifle built so special that it has to be supported on a bench and loaded with ammunition so vulnerable to dirt, weather or unintentional disassembly that I can't carry the stuff. Although my eyes have long since passed their peak of perfection, I won't carry a rifle in the woods that doesn't have a set of iron sights on it sighted in for the ammo I'm using.

A rifle and ammunition that will gnaw a single ragged hole in the middle of the target is of little use to me unless I can use that same ammo to drive the bullet into a deer's flank with the positive knowledge it will range forward through the chest and out the neck. Holes in paper don't put meat on the table no matter how close together they are.

In my early days I was happy with a rifle that would handle factory ammunition. Since 1949, however, I haven't shot a single head of game with a factory-loaded centerfire cartridge, and today I'm not interested in any rifle for which I cannot make the bullets, preferably paper patched bullets.

I use a benchrest for testing rifles and ammunition and for sighting-in purposes. For practice in the hunting field, however, there is nothing better than stand-up, hind-leg shooting from a hunting stance, not the elbow-on-hip, flat-palm stance used in competition. For a practice target, I often use the 500-meter ram silhouette painted on a sheet of corrugated board, and I shoot a load that gives enough recoil to let me know I'm using a rifle. Just as I couldn't use .45-70 practice to familiarize myself with the flintlock, neither can I use a .22 rimfire as substitute practice for the .45-70.

I like fixed power scopes and have never owned but one variable power scope in my life — an early model Weaver KV purchased in 1952. Not only do I want a fixed power scope, I want a scope of 2½ or 3x that is short, lightweight and rugged. For my .375 H&H and my Ruger No. 3 .30-40, I go to 4x because of the rifle's longer range capability. I see no earthly use for more than 4x in the hunting field, and it makes little sense to me to take a beautiful, easy-handling, lightweight rifle and bog it down with a heavy, bulky 3x9 variable.

For sighting in and ammo testing, I have targets printed with a three-inch black square enclosing a two-inch white square. The target suits my purposes, although with my present eyesight when using a 2½x scope, I'm really aiming at the paper's center.

Right, wrong or indifferent that is my way of doing things. Others do it differently. Fred Cornell's idea of a testing target is to use a large sheet of white paper or poster board with a single red thumbtack in the center. And don't be surprised if that thumbtack disappears!

I nearly fell over the day we went to the shooting range to test his .45-caliber slug rifle for the first time, and he put up his target with the thumbtack center. Yet, when I sat down behind that rifle and peered through the 20x Unertl scope, it all made sense. Like Fred says, you can't hit what you can't see, and with that big scope perched atop a 17½-pound rifle, I could quarter the head of the thumbtack with room to spare.

Bob Gillan is the finest rifle shot I've ever known (and an even better pistol shot) with a strong liking for the old cartridges and rifles. He has a keen sense for iron sights and is a superb offhand shot, better than I ever was or will be. Yet our views on what is required of a rifle sometimes are quite different. If Bob gets a rifle that won't shoot the garden variety of ammunition, he gets rid of the rifle. To me, such a rifle is a challenge to find out why it won't shoot and then to learn what will make it shoot.

That is the way we learn, an exchange of vastly different ideas, the curiosity to know why and quite often a backward step in time to find out how the old-timers made bullets with paper jackets and how they worked.

Although those on the outside may look at a rifle and see only an instrument of death, those of us on the inside recognize it for what it really is, the pinnacle of man's efforts toward his own personal protection and welfare, the instrument by which he started his first march toward personal freedom, the one inanimate object upon which a man can turn personal affection with the knowledge that the rifle will respond in kind.

The American Heritage — may we always be free to own and use them!

Other Books
by
Paul A. Matthews

The Paper Jacket
Forty Years with the .45-70
Paul Matthews' Ben and the Old Man

Available from:
Wolfe Publishing Company
6471 Airpark Drive
Prescott, Arizona 86301